P9-CDH-453

PRAISE FOR

NEVER SIT IF YOU CAN DANCE

"Stories about life, about love, about family. When she was younger, Jo didn't understand her mother. When she was older, Jo realized how smart, how special her mother was. You choose the heroine. I choose both."
—ILENE BECKERMAN, author of *Love, Loss, and What I Wore*

"You could read this book on one plane flight—and leave with the satisfying feeling you have been traveling with a delightful, memorable companion."
—RENA PEDERSON, author of *The Burma Spring*

"Babe is a life-embracing role model for anyone seeking to make their days dance with love and joy."
—ELIZABETH FORSYTHE HAILEY, author of *A Woman of Independent Means*

"Babe's lessons are simple, but each is a valuable gem. Her lifelong zest for squeezing pleasure from just about everything is heartwarming and entertaining."
—CAROL SALINE, author of *Mothers & Daughters*

"From arm-wrestling to thank-you notes, this breezy tribute from a feminist to her old-fashioned mom celebrates both civility and love."
—LESLIE LEHR, author of *What a Mother Knows*

"This snappy mother-daughter memoir brings old-fashioned lessons to life with a clever and modern twist."

—LINDA GRAY SEXTON, *New York Times* best-selling author of *Searching for Mercy Street*

"We all need a Babe in our lives! Lucky for Jo Giese having hers, and lucky for us that she's sharing her with us in this uplifting romp through one woman's well-lived life. You'll laugh, you'll cry, and then you'll want to read it all over again just to get a little more Babe."

—NANCY SPILLER, author of *Compromise Cake: Lessons Learned from My Mother's Recipe Box*

NEVER SIT
IF YOU
CAN DANCE

Lessons from My Mother

JO GIESE

SHE WRITES PRESS

Copyright © 2019 by Jo Giese

All rights reserved. No part of this publication may be reproduced, distributed, or transmitted in any form or by any means, including photocopying, recording, digital scanning, or other electronic or mechanical methods, without the prior written permission of the publisher, except in the case of brief quotations embodied in critical reviews and certain other noncommercial uses permitted by copyright law. For permission requests, please address She Writes Press.

Published April 23, 2019
Printed in the United States of America
Print ISBN: 978-1-63152-533-9
E-ISBN: 978-1-63152-534-6
Library of Congress Control Number: 2018957236

For information, address:
She Writes Press
1563 Solano Ave #546
Berkeley, CA 94707

Interior design by Tabitha Lahr

She Writes Press is a division of SparkPoint Studio, LLC.

In memory of my parents.
I'm so sorry they didn't hang around longer
so we could have grown old together.

CONTENTS

INTRODUCTION

One day Babe and I were discussing why some people we knew were so unhappy and cranky. I asked her, "Okay, so why do you think I turned out so happy?"

"Because you take after me," she said.

That's when the idea of *Never Sit If You Can Dance* was born. I'd been a seventies-bell-bottom-wearing, *Ms.* magazine-writing daughter who was sorely disappointed with my stay-at-home-housewife mom. She seemed so behind the times. I'd look at her and think, *Lord, I do not want to turn out like* that!

But, half a century later, this baby boomer has lived long enough to realize how seriously I underestimated her. Maybe we weren't members of such different generations after all. She might have had stewed rhubarb and tomato aspic salad in her fridge, while I have organic kale and soy milk in mine, but maybe, in more important ways, we're much closer in spirit than I thought. And at ninety-five and a half, she'd put up with me long enough to hear me start singing her praises publicly in a Houston magazine.

I called Mom "Babe" because she asked me to—she disliked her given name, Gladys. Besides, Babe was fun to say, and it suited her. She was the youngest in her family, the baby. But even after she'd outlived three sisters, her husband, and everybody else, the name still fit. She was some Babe.

I'm especially delighted that in this Instagram age, a woman who never touched a computer or owned a cell phone or played solitaire on an iPad had wisdom—earned from a lifetime of living—that has turned out to be timeless.

Probably nobody is more surprised than I am that, stitch by stitch, I embroidered Babe's pronouncements into life lessons. And many of these lessons weren't necessarily even spoken until we sat down together, and I asked about all that dancing she and Dad had done. That's when she blurted out, "Never sit if you can dance."

If I've been successful, I've communicated her grace, her wit, and her playfulness. ("Let's goof off today" was one of her favorite sayings.) Taken together, these lessons show there's a celebratory life waiting for each of us—*if* we embrace it.

As you come to know Babe, you'll see that she was no Goody Two-Shoes. She drank, danced, and stayed up *very* late. She was so much livelier than most mothers I've known. And since I frown on manuals telling me which fork or word to use, this is *not* that. Instead, these lessons, defined by love, rather than by prohibition, are stories about what worked pretty well for Babe. They are about the simplest, most basic things: how to get along with other people, how to make a marriage work, how to make life more agreeable.

I got such a kick out of focusing on Babe that I had no intention of having much of a presence in these pages myself. But as her stories unfolded, they naturally evolved into mother-daughter stories. How could they not? And, again, why should I have been so surprised? Because Babe's lessons show not just how she lived, but the impact her attitudes and ideas had on me and the others lucky enough to have known her.

It's been said that our gifts are not fully ours until we give them away. I wrote this collection as a gift for Babe and for all mothers everywhere who laid the groundwork that shaped us, even if we didn't exactly recognize it or appreciate it—or them—at the time. Babe gave me these gifts, and in this book, I'm giving them to you.

LESSON 1:

NEVER SIT
IF YOU CAN DANCE

Neither of my parents pursued any activity that today would qualify as exercise. Theirs was many generations before Jane Fonda's "feel the burn!" workout videos, before isometrics and aerobics, before Lululemon and Under Armour, before they even knew that regular exercise was good for them. And, as my father would have told you, he was too damn busy making a buck to take up idle, elitist pursuits—like tennis, golf, or, God forbid, skiing—that are a waste of time, not to mention money. Whizzing down a mountain on boards—what's the point of *that*?

Babe's specialty was the standing backbend. Although I never saw her execute one, she explained that she'd put her fingers on the wall behind her and climb down the wall backward. "My back was flexible," she said. "That was my most important exercise."

And she could arm-wrestle. It's curious how someone so ladylike, someone who preferred blouses with ruffles, didn't look anything like a wrestler, and never honed her skill with wrist-strengthening exercises would invite anyone to a bout. In between hands of pinochle or gin rummy, she'd challenge someone new, and it had to be someone who wasn't wise to her trick. She'd push her cards aside, place her right elbow on the card table at a ninety-degree angle, fist up, place her left hand across her upper arm to steady it, lock it with her opponent's, and—*wham!*—before they knew what had happened, their wrist would be pinned down to the table, and Babe would bask in another moment of glory. Take *that*, Jane Fonda. The success of her trick relied on the element of surprise, coupled with a natural technique in which she leveraged the strength in her shoulder. And Babe—who had no gym routine, no personal trainer, no arm-wrestling coach—always won.

Years later, as I lifted free weights to maintain what bicep-forearm strength I had, Babe's naturally powerful grip puzzled me. But then maybe I was puzzled by Babe's many strengths in general. Her physical stamina—and not just with arm-wrestling—amazed me. How she could stay up so late, as long as there were friends to socialize with, while I was an early-to-bed, early-to-rise person who was happiest when I could also sneak in a delicious afternoon nap? I was a napper; Babe never napped.

The only exercise Dad mentioned was jumping jacks in the sixth grade, and it was those jumping jacks that cut his education short. Very short. According to Dad, the teacher, who was a man, yelled at him, criticizing how he was executing the jumping jacks.

"If the instructor didn't think you were doing it right," said Dad, "or doing your best, he had kids bend down and touch the floor, and he'd whack 'em. Hell, I was about as big as him—maybe a little bigger. If he was gonna whack me, I'd whack him." Dad resisted hitting the teacher and instead exited that elementary school, and never returned. (Though later in life, as a self-trained engineer, he felt hamstrung by having shortchanged his education.)

Just because Dad lacked formal training, educational or otherwise, didn't mean he was physically inactive. Every Christmas he'd climb the tallest evergreen tree in our backyard in Seattle—it was at least two or three stories high—and top it off with a five-pointed star outlined in white lights. Imagine my dad—six feet tall, thirty-five years old, muscular but bare-bones skinny because, as he said, he ate to live, rather than living to eat—scaling those prickly Douglas-fir branches. First he found a toehold; then he placed a foot there, found another branch to perch on, grabbed a handhold, and hoisted himself up—all while carrying that huge star and dragging a long extension cord while as Perry Como crooned carols from an outdoor speaker: "I'm dreaming of a white Christmas. . . ."

His nervous wife and his two little kids were staring up from way down below. And now I wonder, how did he know how to do *that*? He certainly never trained on any indoor climbing wall. If my husband, Ed, or I attempted such a feat, we'd break our ankle before we reached the first branch. (As crazy-scary as that incident was, it imprinted me for life: Christmas isn't Christmas without lights outside. And whenever we hang lights—or a more agile friend hangs them for us—there must be holiday music blaring loudly, the cornier the better. Our lights end up looking hokey and just right.)

My parents didn't even know how to swim, except in a pinch Dad could dog-paddle. But, boy, could they dance.

One of my favorite black-and-white photos from a family scrapbook was of my parents dressed up to attend a dance at the Washington Athletic Club in their courtship days. Mom was wearing a graceful black, floor-length gown, an unusual choice for someone who clearly favored color. At twenty-seven, she probably thought it made her look sophisticated, and it did. That languid dress was clingy enough to show some curves, and her auburn hair was done in deep finger waves, a flirty hairstyle that was popular back then. Dad was wearing a black tuxedo. Imagine that: Dad—who ended up favoring one-piece, baby-blue polyester jumpsuits from Penney's—at thirty, and courting Babe, was dressed to kill in a gorgeous black tuxedo. That photo captured a man and a woman who were clearly a hot couple. They looked so fresh and young, so glamorous and romantic, so pre-children. Since Babe had also told me that Dad sometimes took a room at the Washington Athletic Club, over the years I nagged her to tell me if she'd ever stayed there with him before they married. "You can tell me, Mom. It'll just be between us." She *never* said. What she did say, which was so disappointing and unsatisfying, was, "I think that's private."

Every Saturday my mom and dad, before they were my mom and dad, went to a dance hall, often the Trianon Ballroom in downtown Seattle. Babe said it was beautiful, with polished hardwood floors, and it was so packed that on Saturday nights you could hardly get in.

"We never went anywhere that didn't have an orchestra. It was first class all the way. You would've liked that place," she said to me.

When I googled the Trianon, which is located in what is now a hipster area north of Seattle called Belltown, I learned that the dance floor had accommodated five *thousand* dancers.

"Pa always had a corsage for me."

"You danced with a corsage?" I said. "Didn't it flop all over the place?"

"Once in a while, but he never came without one."

Babe said that everyone in their crowd was a dancer, a smooth dancer, and they danced to beautiful music, not the "junk" people listen to today. If, as the saying goes, dancing is sex standing up, then my parents and their friends must have had a really good erotic time gliding around those beautiful ballrooms.

Her crowd did the foxtrot, the swing, the two-step, but nothing jumpy like the jitterbug or boogie-woogie. Babe said that sometimes the dance hall had a Charleston contest—"but we weren't Charleston people."

Their marriage and the arrival of my brother, Jimmy, and me coincided with the passing of the big-band era and the closing of the dance halls, but our parents kept dancing. At home. Babe and Dad were a popular couple, and by then they had the largest house in their group—not large by current standards, but big enough by post-World War II, 1950's, middle-class standards—so the parties were always at our place. Dad had turned a daylight basement into a rec room with a highly waxed, green linoleum dance floor that he'd glued down tile by tile using a disgusting, black, tar-like adhesive. That danceable space was where my brother and I skidded around in our stocking feet, and where I cradled my new baby sister, Wendy, as I danced her to sleep. That's also where the adults— young couples with young children, hardworking and hard-partying—danced and drank and smoked and celebrated into the wee hours. That was my instructional template for being a grown-up: gather a bunch of friends, some aunts and uncles, coworkers, and neighbors; roll up the rugs; and drink and dance.

"Your dad and I definitely never sat and just drank alcohol," said Babe.

"Well, so what did you do, if you didn't just sit and drink?" I asked, reverting to my best professional interview style. Neither of my parents were easy to interview; they would glare at me, knowing I already knew the answer. But I needed them to say it in their own words.

"*We danced!*" she said, as if I were an idiot for even asking. "Never sit if you can dance."

When Herb Alpert and his trumpet blasted onto the scene with the Tijuana Brass and *The Lonely Bull*, Babe wore a bias-cut, flared taffeta skirt, which she'd sewn herself, that swayed when she danced to "Whipped Cream" and "A Taste of Honey." By then Dad had installed a handy beer keg in the kitchen, and the adults stayed up even later.

Babe and Dad's party drugs of choice were drinking and dancing—D & D. Dave Barry, in writing about his parents drinking and partying, said, "My parents and their friends probably would have lived longer if their lifestyle choices had been healthier." As you'll see, Babe lived a *very* long and full life, and she and her friends worked hard, played hard, and had a lot of fun. What's healthier than that, Dave?

I pretty much caught Babe's sassy sense of rhythm and enthusiasm for dancing: in elementary school I raced home to dance with Dick Clark's *American Bandstand* on our black-and-white TV.

That was also when my least favorite aunt, the one who'd worked her entire life as a secretary at the Trick & Murray office supply store, got tickets for the two of us to attend the Elvis Presley concert at the Seattle Rainiers' baseball stadium. How Aunt Dell, of all people, got those tickets, and just a few rows back, I'll never know. When Elvis took the stage in person, right in front of us, with that lock of dark hair falling over his eye and his guitar slung suggestively over his pelvis, and sang "Hound Dog," the place went wild. Like everyone else in that packed stadium, my Aunt Dell and I stood on our chairs and *screamed*. As Elvis gyrated his hips to "Don't Be Cruel," we jumped up and down and danced in the aisles.

I never saw Aunt Dell so uninhibited and joyous. Often she had a sour frown on her face, and she usually complained to her sister, Babe, when they went out, "Why is everyone giving *you* compliments?" It was only after reading *Dancing in the Streets*, by Barbara Ehrenreich, that I understood my aunt's one-time transformation. Ehrenreich had been writing about teenage girls at rock-and-roll concerts, but she might as well have been writing about Aunt Dell: "The crowd mania unleashed something in girls who individually might have been timid and obedient."

By my freshman year at the University of Texas, during the legendary Texas-OU weekend celebrating one of the biggest rivalries in college football, I was having crazy fun at a fraternity party. The first in my family to go to college, there I was, down on all fours on a beer-soaked dance floor, "gatoring" to the Grateful Dead's "Gloria." I'm not sure that's what Babe had in mind when she advised, "Never sit if you can dance."

Being Babe's daughter, I guess it should be no surprise that in stressful transitions I turned to dancing. During the divorce from my first husband, the one I only refer to as the "bad husband," and the one about whom I never reveal how long we were together because it makes me look like such a slow learner, I line-danced. I ended up so dizzy from twirling and spinning that I had to excuse myself from the line to gather my bearings and catch my breath. But I was grateful for the self-loss, and the self-rescuing I experienced dancing with a line of strangers.

After the death of my second husband, the man who thought I was lovable and whom I believed, I signed up for swing lessons with the Dance Doctor in Santa Monica. But the lessons were too decorously choreographed, too contained, too formal, too much like following doctor's orders—*foot-ball-change*—and in high heels. I craved something—*else!*

That's when I stumbled upon Fumbling Toward Ecstasy, on Sunday mornings—a time slot I was having trouble filling. Fumbling turned out to be improvisational, trancelike group dancing, also called 5Rhythms. In a large warehouse transformed into a dance space, I entered another world—a feverish world—where hundreds of people gathered to dance for the dance of it. After seventeen years of a good marriage that was now gone, I clung to Fumbling to escape being isolated in my too-silent house with only one small dog (sorry, Charmlee) for company. It was always high-quality entertainment—a woman in a pink leotard was an awe-inspiring professional dancer, a Chinese man in an orange, ankle-length, pleated skirt glided by as smoothly as an ice skater, and a belly dancer was swathed in layers of purple edged with tinkling bells and bangles. Since I had no idea what I was doing, I appreciated it when the director said to me, "Anyone can fumble. You can't get it 'wrong.'"

One of my nephews asked, "Is that like a Sunday-morning rave? A mosh pit for adults?" Maybe, I said.

Sometimes the music was cranked up so loud that I was transported back to the craziness of frat parties at UT. But those were called Friday-night keg parties, not Sunday-morning trance dancing. I was so thrilled with Fumbling that I even took Babe. By then she was in her late eighties, and I got her a chair so she could watch from the sidelines or join in if she wanted to. Afterward she said she didn't understand why people didn't dance with partners, or why some men—some of them wearing long skirts—danced with each other. She wasn't judgmental, just puzzled.

Flash forward. I no longer spent my Sunday mornings dancing like a dervish, and Babe was no longer dancing. In her nineties, she was walker-bound, and she was not reconciled to her fate. One day when we were going through the old photos, we came across that dreamy one of her and Dad before they went dancing. "I'd give anything if I could dance," she said. "My feet aren't suitable now."

Although Babe had managed to avoid all major health problems, she suffered from peripheral neuropathy, a nerve disorder where she lost feeling on the soles of her feet, an ironic malady to beset someone who had loved to dance. The condition destroyed her balance and created an urgent need for her to cling to her walker. Since the walker was red, we called it her Ferrari.

"People should dance more and sit less," she said.

I told her that her gorgeous Trianon Ballroom had been converted into an office building.

"That's kind of awkward," she said.

I wondered if any of the office workers at the Trianon on Third Avenue in Seattle knew they were working in what had once been one of the largest dance halls west of Chicago, the kind where giant mirrored balls rotated on the ceiling and couples fell in love.

I did not tell Babe that all signs of her popular dance club were long gone, and that the historic Trianon dance hall now housed a gym.

When Ed and I married in 2009, I asked Babe to walk me down the aisle. Dad had died years earlier, so Babe, my only living parent, was the natural choice.

"You'd better ask someone else," she said. At ninety-two, she was turning me down. "I don't know if I can."

"Of course you can," I said, trusting her lifetime of resiliency and spunk.

The "aisle" was a dirt path on a rugged mountaintop at a nature preserve located in the Santa Monica Mountains. The afternoon of the wedding, some of Ed's six grandchildren, dressed in colorful cotton wedding sweaters, flew kites from the windy mountaintop. I wore a red bridal gown (see Lesson 10: Don't Be Drab) with a train that a friend said fluttered in the breeze like a flame. The beautiful mother of the bride was dressed elegantly in a hot-pink Chinese coat with a mandarin collar. Her Ferrari was decorated with so many colorful flowers, it looked like a moving bouquet.

After the flower girls scattered petals down the aisle, and the ring bearers made their way to the canopy where Ed, the groom, was waiting, the string quartet struck up "Penny Lane." A gasp passed through the crowd as our friends realized that Babe *was* walking me down the aisle. Everyone stood and cheered and clapped. And Babe—never sit if you can dance—danced at my wedding.

LESSON 2:

MAYBE WE ALL NEED
SOMEONE WAITING FOR US
IN THE PARKING LOT

My dad's business was headquartered—if "head-quartered" can be used to describe the warehouse offices of such a small, scrappy enterprise—in what was then the grimy, industrial waterfront section of West Seattle. Dad had learned his area of specialty by sand-blasting ships in the Bremerton shipyard during World War II. From hard-earned, firsthand knowledge, he knew what equipment was missing in shipyards, and he thought he knew how to design it better. Later, as the inventor and manufacturer of this new equipment, he made sales trips up and down the coast—from Anacortes to Astoria, Seaside to San Francisco.

By then my grandmother Josie was living with us and could take care of my brother and me. So Babe, who was also the bookkeeper for Dad's fledging business, often went on the road with him. While Dad was inside, shooting the breeze, trying to convince the buyer at Todd Shipyard in Portland that his equipment would overhaul, clean, and dry-dock their ships better and faster, Babe was outside in the car, doing needlework.

Babe always brought along a basket crammed with the supplies she needed for her pastime: packets of needles, thimbles, wooden hoops that kept the fabric taut, twists of the thinnest embroidery thread in a rainbow of colors, tiny scissors for snipping off the ends, and a stash of projects—dish towels, pillowcases, a tablecloth—most with pre-stenciled designs.

"It's a nice pastime, and when you finish, you have an accomplishment," Babe explained years later. She did *not* do it for the meditative, calming quality of stitch in, stitch out, breathe in, breathe out, which is what I did years later when I took up needlepoint. "I didn't need any calm down stuff," she said. "I liked the results. I was always anxious to get through to see what it looked like."

I wondered if she ever encouraged her sisters, Evie and Dell, or any of her many friends, especially the women in her pinochle club, to take up embroidery. "I enjoyed doing it myself, but other people I knew didn't like doing it. Too much work and not enough praise."

That wasn't the whole story. In 1940, her sister Evie cross-stitched a "home sweet home" pictorial, and in 1934, Babe's oldest friend from kindergarten, Thelma, created a miniature needlework diptych of two houses. I know this because those pieces hang in my home. But probably Babe was right about their not liking it much, because, as far as I know, those pieces were their only output.

On those road trips with Dad, as Babe waited outside in industrial parking lots, she embroidered. It might have been a precisely stitched set of pillowcases that would get finished with a lacy edge crocheted by my grandmother, who also spun pastel doilies as fine as a spiderweb. Or she might embroider a dish towel that was signed by the artist, MOM, in large block letters.

"That was when people had dish towels hanging out," she said. "I stopped that some time ago. Too much work for what they're worth."

More than a decade before Gloria Steinem and Betty Friedan, I looked down on what I saw as Babe's silly, subservient behavior. A French knot here, a fly stitch there, and Babe—who wasn't a perfectionist about anything else—was such a perfectionist about her needlework that she proudly showed off the front *and* back of the fabric. But what difference did it make if she was so skillful you couldn't tell the topside from the underside of a dish towel? I mean, really—surely, there was something more important for this person to be doing than perfecting French knots. To my little eight-year-old judgmental self, who sometimes got to tag along on these trips, Dad was up to something important, exciting, inside—a business meeting—while Babe was outside *stitching*?

Back then, I had almost no exposure to professional women, other than the teachers at school; or Mandy, our neighbor who was a nurse; or Aunt Evie, who was in the Women's Army Corps. Although Evie was my favorite aunt, her job—as a glorified office worker—didn't impress me much, either. But at least she got to wear an olive-green army uniform with a matching tie, and a cap she tilted at a jaunty angle. I have no idea where these judgmental (and aspirational) ideas came from, and I'm not sure what I thought Babe should be doing instead. But I was pretty sure what she should *not* be doing: needlework while waiting for Dad. It seemed so docile and passive.

Many years later when I was talking to Babe about this, she said, "Your dad always told me how nice it was to come out to the car and have someone to talk to."

Oh.

Babe, the crafter, out there doing raised French knots—stitch in, stitch out, tie it off—had been an active participant in a way that I, the little put-down artist, had never given her credit for. I'd never considered the important supporting role she'd been playing all those years in bolstering her husband and in strengthening their marriage. Dad was a talented but self-taught engineer who had to hire a licensed engineer to sign off on his designs. Though he didn't like to let on, his lack of formal education had left him with feelings of inferiority. What a deep comfort it must have been to have his wife waiting for him. Maybe his meeting hadn't gone well and he'd lost a sale. He would come out dejected, and Babe could console him. And when he felt like a million bucks, he had someone to celebrate with. If Willy Loman had had a Babe to kick back with, and laugh with, and have a scotch and soda with after his sales calls, how different his story might have been.

I couldn't help but think of all the times I'd been on the road without anyone waiting in the car for me. Once, I was interviewing the groundskeeper for the Detroit Tigers—it was a wonderful public radio story about the first woman groundskeeper in major league baseball and how she'd worked her way up from the minors—but I ended up stuck by myself, working on the script, over a long, lonely weekend in a hotel in a questionable area of downtown Detroit. Boy, what a difference it would have made if I'd had someone like Babe.

Mom and Dad didn't need to drive all the way to the Pasadena Auditorium, like I did, to listen to His Holiness the Dalai Lama lecture about the interdependence of all sentient beings, and take notes, and underline key passages with a yellow highlighter. Their common thread was that they had no false ideas about the value of independence. They were not afraid to lean in. There was no stigma attached—except by one scoldy daughter.

Then the seventies hit, and the counterculture age of free love, flower children, and colorful embroidery burst onto the scene. From denim shirts to designer dresses, all the cool clothing was splashed with high-impact embroidery. Embroidery had acquired fashion chops. I eyed Babe's handiwork with new, greedy eyes. For my sister and me, she embroidered gorgeous, vibrant flowers on our favorite work shirts, and long, leafy stems that spiraled down the sides of our jeans. Babe's talent, unleashed from those quiet dish towels and dainty pillowcases, exploded onto our hip clothing. Now she used chunkier threads, in thicker stitches, and the sculptural result resembled a three-dimensional tapestry. Her unbridled work was richer and more complicated than the mass-produced versions. Take *that*, Ralph Lauren.

Babe's largest and longest embroidery project— it took her *years* to complete—was a tablecloth big enough for a wedding. "Banquet size," she said. The white linen fabric featured a central oval with spokes of rose-colored, daisy-like flowers on delicate, pale gray stems with wisps of light blue leaves. Its subtle, sophisticated palette—no yellow daisies with green leaves for Babe—matched her Haviland china.

"It's a pretty thing, isn't it?" she said. It was December 2012, and I'd just spread her treasure on the table for Christmas dinner.

Babe's masterpiece—which boasts hundreds and hundreds of embroidered flowers, each with a pale blue, perfectly executed French knot in its center—also has matching napkins. "I wound up giving it to you," she said, "my oldest daughter."

Babe was among a legion of unsung women embroiderers of her generation. These needleworkers, who practiced a lost art, rarely received any formal public recognition for their painstakingly crafted pieces. No one collected Babe's artwork except my sister and me.

My husband, formerly a whip-smart appellate lawyer in Washington, DC, who had argued many cases at the Supreme Court, said, "I was always litigating issues that you'd read about in the newspapers. But what's really the long-term impact? Who's to say that work is any more valuable than your mom's tablecloth?"

When there's yet another wildfire scare in the area where we live, and we go into adrenaline overdrive, scanning the mountains for telltale signs of fire, getting out the suitcases, and the very real possibility of evacuation looms in the smoky air, the first treasure I grab is Babe's tablecloth.

Today, in an era that stresses individual self-fulfillment and achievement, hardly anyone is willing to be the one sitting in the car, stitching. But the simple truth is that maybe we all need someone waiting for us in the parking lot.

LESSON 3:

NEVER SHOW UP
EMPTY-HANDED

B abe was a child of the original Great Depression, and, although times were tight, she wasn't.

My parents would always arrive at a friend's house with their arms loaded. "It's a nice way of welcoming yourself into someone's home," Babe explained. "Be sure and bring something you've made, too." She might bring a bowl of her homemade clam dip or a Pyrex baking dish of scalloped potatoes—modest 1950's food. Dad would usually bring a bottle of booze. They *always* brought flowers, fresh flowers.

It was unthinkable, impossible, to show up empty-handed.

My parents had started off married life in Ballard, in northwestern Seattle, where they lived and worked in a two-story shop: Dad sandblasted cars on the first floor, and Mom and Dad and the two kids lived upstairs. ("There was money in sandblasting cars if you did it right," Babe explained. "And of course Pa did it right. The train ran right through our property day and night. It was a business property.") Back in the 1940s, they were scraping by, living for two years in an industrial building with aluminum siding until they had the opportunity to sell that building and move out into a cute little redbrick starter house. Today, that industrial loft would qualify as sought-after, hipster housing.

Later, when I was an adult, I wondered if their generosity was also tinged with a bit of overcompensatory behavior, at least on my father's part. For someone who'd had such a challenging childhood—his mother was only fourteen when he was born, a mere child herself—he started off behind. So when he arrived loaded with gifts, couldn't that have helped make a good first impression and pave the way for a warm reception?

A Croatian friend told me about *slatko*: in a Serbian home, the host greets guests at the front door, holding a silver tray lined with a lace doily, and offers them a spoonful of rose-petal jam in a glass of water to sweeten the visit. I enjoyed imagining my generous parents, laden with their goodies, being welcomed into such a household, each person sweetening the visit with their own rituals of hospitality.

Being my parents' daughter, I, too, learned to err on the side of generosity. Not lavish, "look at me" generosity but—I hope—friendly, thoughtful generosity. Is it possible to take this generosity business too far, though? A few years back, I tutored a homeless boy, and, although Bobby was in the sixth grade and already sprouting a faint mustache, he had the reading comprehension of a young elementary-school child. However, he excelled in one area: he could draw. Bobby had inherited this ability from his father, an artist who created custom-made medical prosthetics in his garage. When my sister, a painter, learned that the boy I tutored had artistic talent, for Christmas she got him one of those snazzy wooden artist boxes, complete with a carrying handle and stocked with oils, acrylics, and watercolors. When I saw the size of the case, I was afraid it would cramp the tiny room, already crammed with two bunk beds, that Bobby shared with his mom and two sisters at the Salvation Army shelter, and I apologized. "Maybe my sister's gone overboard—"

"Overboard's good!" Bobby grinned. As he walked back into the shelter, carrying his huge wooden case, I swear he seemed taller.

For Babe, overboard was also cool; underboard, not so much. An unfortunate aspect of this family legacy is that when a guest shows up empty-handed, I struggle not to be small-minded and resentful, as in, *How dare she breeze in here without even a tulip for the hostess?*

"Which is probably a little unfair," says Ed.

It's fascinating what family rituals we drag around with us and expect others to know and respect. And, boy, if they don't . . . Of course, a guest might send something afterward, backloading the experience. But since Babe so enthusiastically favored the frontloading approach, so do I.

I don't know that she would have felt the sting so sharply, or would have been pleased to know that her oldest daughter took her "don't show up empty-handed" guideline so much to heart. But it requires some mental jiggering to remind myself that this perfectly nice person who just arrived empty-handed for a long weekend, for whom I've stocked the refrigerator with her favorite coconut milk and the pantry with her gluten-free breakfast cereal, probably isn't cheap or selfish or thoughtless. She just didn't have Babe for a mom.

LESSON 4:

THANK-YOU NOTES ARE NEVER TOO PLENTIFUL

Babe was such a stickler about thank-you notes that it seems like I was barely out of the womb when I got my first little box of dime-store stationery. Under her tutelage, I felt as if I had to start writing the thank-you while I was still ripping off the wrapping paper, and I resented it.

"Thank-you notes are never too plentiful. That's the whole thing in a nutshell," Babe explained.

I was amused to read that the handwritten thank-you note—that seemingly antiquated custom that was commonplace in Babe's generation—is very much alive and well in the digital age, even among millennials. That would not have surprised Babe. She could have told you it's the little things that count, big-time, and don't go out of style.

Stop and think of the pleasure you feel when you receive a slow, handwritten thank-you versus a fast, thumb-typed "*thnks!*"

And when you write a thank-you, you don't need to drool or get all touchy-feely. Just a few nicely worded one-liners will do the job. Like the one Babe sent after joining us for our anniversary weekend: "My dear Ed and Jo: You have a beautiful home. Thank you for sharing. All my love to you two love-birds. Mom/Babe."

Good thank-you notes make the recipients feel good about themselves. They did something cool, and someone noticed.

Babe's idea of expressing appreciation by writing thank-yous was reinforced by Dad, who, in one unfortunate incident, took Mom's maxim to a new low. Back then, the best department store in Seattle was Frederick & Nelson, and getting a present from that fancy establishment was a rare treat. One day when I was about eight, my parents came home with a huge gift-wrapped box from that special store.

For *me*? For me.

I undid the bow, tore open the paper, lifted the lid, and found, lying there in layers of tissue, a coat. A purple winter coat. As far as I was concerned, it might as well have been a huge, slimy slug.

"I *hate* purple," I said, with unconcealed disappointment.

"It's not purple," said Babe, the family peace-keeper. "It's maroon."

"I won't wear it."

"Toots," my dad fumed, "you'll wear it and like it!"

Sensing my sinking spirits and seeking to quell the rising conflict, Babe explained that it had been on sale, so there was no returning it. But Dad wouldn't have taken it back anyway. As far as he was concerned, any child of his was damn lucky to have a new, warm winter coat—of any color, any size. (He felt the same way about food—parsnips, rutabagas, turnips—which made for some tense meals.)

"Try it on," Babe urged.

Reluctantly, I slipped it on. The sleeves were so long they hung over my hands. I didn't bother to button it. "I don't like it," I said, slumping my shoulders. I had no intention of growing into it.

"We went to great effort to get you this present," said Babe.

"Sister, you'll learn to be grateful. Or else," said my dad. Years later, I realized he must have been so bent out of shape because when he was a child he'd probably never gotten a new coat, only hand-me-downs. On the spot, he invented my punishment. I had to write the sentence "I will be grateful for everything I get" one thousand times.

"That's not fair!" I whined.

Every day after school, the little ingrate, a golden

blonde (then a natural blonde) with curly ringlets (then natural curls), trudged downstairs to the card table in the basement, where she labored in the coal mines of that sentence. Since she was just progressing from block printing to cursive, and she gripped her #2 pencil extra hard, you can imagine how long it took her to eke out that sentence, even thirty-one times, enough to fill just one page of lined newsprint.

Time crept by in slow motion. The delicious, yeasty aroma of her favorite Parker House dinner rolls, which her grandmother was baking upstairs, wafted downstairs, as well as the extra loud, happy shrieks of her brother and his friend, who were rubbing it in that they were playing upstairs while she was being punished downstairs.

You can bet she was not thinking, *I'm learning gratitude.* It was more like, *This is not fair! I'm stuck down here in the basement, my hand's cramping, my finger's getting a callus, and I hate my father.*

When Babe was in her nineties, I was telling her about having to write the longest thank-you note in history, and she interrupted, "You never had to write a thousand. You got to stop at five hundred." I guess I should have been grateful for *that*. Babe also explained that I had a mind of my own, and I was going to use it. She said I was a smart aleck, and that was why I got the most discipline. Oh. (I guess that also explains why I got my mouth washed out with Fels-Naptha laundry soap.)

Looking back on that experience, I can't help but think what a wasted learning opportunity that was, making me write exactly the same sentence over and over and over: "I will be grateful for everything I get." Was that really the best way to develop a child's gratitude muscle? I was just beginning to compose stories and submit them to *Junior Scholastic* magazine—I was working on one about a girl taking ice-skating lessons who was lonely. (Guess who was taking ice-skating lessons and was lonely?) What if my parents had suggested instead that I write about all the people, events, foods, and pets I was grateful for? Wouldn't that have been a more creative use of my time, a more worthwhile teachable moment for a budding wordsmith?

Toward the end of Dad's life, when he was visiting me for what turned out to be the last time, one day at lunch he said, "Can you ever forgive me for making you write those sentences?" He didn't have to say *which* sentences. My father was of that generation of men who did not express their feelings freely, yet the unfairness of that stiff punishment had gnawed at him for half a century.

"Dad, I forgave you a long time ago." His relief was visible. I didn't add that it had taken years of expensive therapy.

Although I seriously doubt that any of the many experts who have shown a link between gratitude and happiness would approve of the way my parents shoved gratitude down my throat, what's weird is that, in its own cocka-mamie way, that screwy punishment worked.

Within that negative wound was the positive gift that I do not take anything for granted. Ever. And I write thank-yous immediately. As my friend Jennie said, "I like giving you presents because no matter what it is, no matter how small, you're so tickled."

This happened again in 2014. I'd bought a small painting of a bear, and I immediately dashed off a quick thank-you to the artist, Robert McCauley, saying his painting was perfect for us, since we'd had a bear in our kitchen in Montana once. He immediately wrote back: "After four decades in mainstream art, I can count on one of my dog's paws the number of people who own my work who have responded in a like manner. You do that with total consciousness. Your thank-you is much appreciated."

Another benefit of this early "discipline" is that years later, when many of my friends were starting to keep gratitude journals, I didn't feel the need to do that. The idea of gratitude had been drilled so deeply into my psyche at such a young age that, as an adult, I do not have to follow any template and write, "I am grateful for _____ because _____."

As my good friend Linda commented, "You are a born appreciator—of everything!" A *born* appreciator. With a little help from Dad.

I regret that in that wrenching moment when Dad asked if I could ever forgive him, I wasn't suf-ficiently aware of the positive impact of what he'd done, so that I could have been more generous and with some tenderness expressed my gratitude to him before he died. That would have been a gift. To him. Thank you, Dad.

LESSON 5:

MAKE THE BEST OF IT

Babe had a lifetime of making the best of it, especially during what might have seemed like the worst of it.

The summer I was twelve, my father's company had a job repairing and replacing the turbines on the Canyon Ferry Dam, located about fifteen miles from Helena, Montana. Business had dried up in the shipyards on the West Coast and was so bad in Seattle, then a one-company town (Boeing), that locals said it was as if Seattle were a window and someone had pulled the shade down.

So that's how we ended up bunking for a summer near the Canyon Ferry Dam. Coming from the rainy, evergreen Pacific Northwest and the lush, wet shores of Lake Washington, it was as though the five of us (now I had a three-year-old sister) had been loaded into a slingshot and—*pow!*—launched into a prickly, dried-up ditch.

In 1898, there had been a general store, a post office, and a ferry on the Missouri River at the dam. But by the time we arrived in 1959, it was a desolate, dusty, godforsaken dump. The main street in downtown Helena was called Last Chance Gulch, and that would have also been a good name for the deserted area near the dam.

In that hardscrabble neck of the woods, which was definitely not your welcoming, big-sky Montana, there was nowhere to live—not one house, no apartments, nothing. Even if you go there today, there's still pretty much nothing, though within sight of the spillway, someone—probably a parks department employee— has added some picnic benches. (Some picnic.) About two miles from the dam, down a remote, deeply rutted, dirt road with no name, Babe found a one-bedroom, one-bath shack to rent. Maybe it had been a miner's cabin, a leftover from the days when the gravel riverbanks of the Missouri had been mined for gold. The place came "furnished" with one scratchy, green, overstuffed couch. (God only knows what had taken place on that couch.) The worn-out linoleum smelled sour and curled up at the edges. The bathroom was so tiny that Babe probably could have stood in the center with her hands on her waist, elbows out, and touched all four walls. She scrubbed and sanitized and scoured the inside of that chicken coop of a shack until it almost sparkled. But there wasn't a thing that could be done about the sad, hard-packed dirt "yard" outside, where random outcroppings of chaparral furnished a cover for rattlesnakes to coil and tumbleweeds to blow by. (By the time I took Ed to visit in 2017, some of the dirt roads in the area had gotten names. Ours was called Cave Gulch. Seemed about right.)

A few down-on-their-luck codgers who lived off the same dead-end road moseyed on by, curious about the new people who were moving in. The men were impressed by Babe's industry and success in cleaning up that dump. One guy asked if she'd spruce up his sorry place. The answer was a polite no.

Somehow Babe crammed a double bed, a bunk bed, and a single into that one bedroom. Now I'm puzzled where she found all those beds out in the middle of nowhere. And did my parents have sex in that room? They had to, right? I mean, we were there for three months. I was your typical hormonally charged, eager-to-buy-my-first-bra, overly inquisitive twelve-year-old. I'd already discovered Babe's diaphragm once (I'd been snooping in the very back of her handkerchief drawer), and I would have been hyperalert to any interesting goings-on under their sheets. Assigned to the upper bunk, I had a perfect aerial view, but I never heard or noticed anything.

At the beginning of that parched, rocky road, off to the right, was a wooden structure that served as a saloon, and that's pretty much where my brother and I hung out, sometimes wearing our swimsuits to stay cool. Even today in rural Montana, where the Wild West is still very much alive, a bartender probably wouldn't let kids while away their days at a bar, but where else were we supposed to go? Besides, there was hardly any cocktail business during the day. Jimmy and I drank A&W root beers while we spun on the barstools, played the pinball machines, and dropped coins in the jukebox—think Paul Anka's "Lonely Boy." Outside, we choked on the dust clouds that got kicked up when a rare vehicle drove by. Thus we passed a slow, hot, dry Montana summer. This was the exact opposite of helicopter parenting. My brother and I were allowed to take a rowboat under the spillway of the dam with no life jackets onboard.

Nowadays, if a husband had a three-month gig in such a hellhole, a place that's never seen a better day, the wife would undoubtedly stay behind with the children in their comfortable home, instead of dragging everyone out to the boonies. Maybe they'd make an obligatory family visit. That wasn't Babe's style. She was crazy about Dad, and where he was, she'd be. We were there to help keep Daddy company. She made the best of it, and so did we.

A few years later, we moved to Houston so Dad could start a new business in a fresh place—remember, the shade was still drawn on Seattle. The move was a huge rupture for Babe. For the first time in her life, she was living away from her hometown, her family, her mother, and her sisters. As Dad explained it, "I couldn't let the family hold me back. My first job was to keep food on the table and a roof over our heads. I saw things falling apart in Seattle, and the more I looked around Houston, the more steel I saw. Shipyards, refineries! I thought, *This is the place for me.*"

But maybe not so much for Babe. We'd hadn't been there long when she got the long-distance phone call that her mother had died. Babe's sisters, Aunt Evie and Aunt Dell, assured their sobbing, inconsolable baby sister that she didn't have to return home for the funeral, which was just as well, since back then people didn't hop on a plane like they do now.

Grandmother Josie died right before Christmas. We'd already shopped for her presents and wrapped them, and Babe had already spent months tenderly embroidering a wall calendar to hang in her room in the nursing home where she lived. (My parents had invited her to move to Houston with us, but by then Josie had fallen and broken her hip and was wheelchair bound.) So Josie never got to open her Christmas presents, never got to see the beautiful linen calendar Babe had worked so hard on, probably thinking of her with every stitch. Mom rolled up that little needlework masterpiece, with our birthdays highlighted in cross-stitching and sparkly sequins, and buried it in the back of her dresser drawer.

She blew her entire inheritance, such as it was, on a used, candy-red, 1960 Ford Sunliner convertible. At the time, we were living in a little rental starter house. Faced with the choice of buying either her first AC window unit or a turquoise area rug, Babe went for the rug and quickly learned about Texas heat and humidity. When money was that tight—rug or AC, AC or rug—it took some spunk to lift your own spirits by splurging on a car.

"A self that goes on changing," wrote Virginia Woolf, "is a self that goes on living." That described Babe. Her mother may have died, but she was going on living.

That summer, she drove my brother, a friend of my brother's, my sister, and me to Seattle to visit her mother's grave. My fourteen-year-old, bikini-wearing self lounged in the sunny backseat (pre-seat belts). I was determined to show up in damp Seattle, where all our relatives were pale, with a Coppertone tan. Babe obliged me by driving with the top down most of the way.

We did place flowers on Josie's grave—a small, simple, solemn granite marker that was level with the closely clipped grass:

JOSEPHINE KENNEY
MOTHER
MAR. 1880–DEC. 1961

Babe had also timed it so that we got to visit the Seattle World's Fair. It's hard to explain how giddy the five of us were as we rode the elevated monorail to the fairground and went up in the Space Needle. *The Space Needle*! It had been on the cover of *LIFE* magazine, and now we were up there. We gorged ourselves on Belgian waffles (with strawberries and cream) and licked at plumes of pink cotton candy as we toured the Science Pavilion and visited the House of the Future.

Now *that's* making the best of a visit to your mother's grave.

What a Babe.

LESSON 6:

SHARING FUN IS
THE WHOLE THING

In 1961, meteorologists in Houston were predicting that the eye of Hurricane Carla, one of the most powerful storms ever to strike the United States, with 175-mile-per-hour winds, was headed for Houston. Texas coastal areas were on an intense hurricane watch. Some people prayed, and some prayed and packed and taped up their windows, just like Dan Rather's colleagues showed us how to do on TV. While we still had power, the news reports reminded us of the deadly hurricane of 1900 that had washed out Galveston and killed about eight thousand people. Along with a half million others, we prepared to evacuate.

The plan was that Babe and her three kids, and Eileen, our next-door-neighbor, and her five kids, would squeeze into Dad's Studebaker. Except when Eileen showed up with all her children *and* her parakeet in its cage *and* a huge jug of water, Babe realized that our neighbor didn't know any more about evacuating than she did.

So our group of potential Hurricane Carla refugees stayed put. Since everyone was stuck in the same situation, with no water and no power, and since Babe had a knack for gathering folks together, in no time most of the neighbors—the McKays from across the street, the Dederers from down the block—had gathered in our living room around a campfire of candles and lanterns.

Hour after hour, as we waited for the hurricane of the century to slam into us, we hung out together, playing board games and eating food, such as we had. "Sharing fun is the whole thing," explained Babe. Carla spent her fury in Galveston. Since I was just twelve and hadn't personally witnessed the total ruination of Galveston, I still savor Waiting for Carla as one of the scariest and friendliest times of my childhood. That crisis, which brought the neighbors together—glued us together in our living room—fulfilled an intense longing for connection.

Years later, I was living in Southern California. A horrific rainstorm that caused mudslides and traffic accidents had closed every road and canyon into and out of our beach community. Since we were stranded, I sloshed over to a neighbor's house—there was no power, no phone service—and invited them to gather around our fire. We'd ride out the storm together.

"It'll be more fun," I said. Things had gotten so bad, it put me in a good mood. Since we were all marooned, the only thing to do was to gather together.

Diane and Fred kept eyeing the door that led from their kitchen to the garage. The bath towels they'd rolled up at the threshold were already sopping wet. My neighbors were too nervous about the heavy rains flooding their house to leave. So I splashed back home, sopping wet, and came back with a platter of sandwiches, which we shared sitting at their dining room table. It wasn't the once-in-a-lifetime community camaraderie of Waiting for Carla—the gathering together of a tribe in a crisis—but it was something.

For Babe, Sharing Fun also meant Celebrate Everything, including May Day. When I was about five, in preparation for the first day of May, I wove little baskets out of strips of paper. Babe and I gathered flowers, rhododendron blooms in shades of pink from our backyard hedge, and stuffed them into the baskets. Then five-year-old me scampered from door to door in the neighborhood, ringing the doorbell, quickly dropping a basket, and running away *fast* (and probably giggling like crazy), before anyone could spot who had left the anonymous Happy May Day gift. As I grew older, I experienced a letdown when it was May 1 and no one was rushing around with May baskets. Once, in my building in New York City, I dropped off small May baskets for the neighbors on our elevator line. For the most part, the gesture was misunderstood. "Isn't May Day International Workers' Day or something like that?" asked a neighbor. Yes, it is that, but it is also a celebration of spring, especially if you're Babe's daughter.

Decades later, Eileen, our next-door neighbor from the Hurricane Carla days, was widowed. She remarried, but since she and her new husband had gotten such a late start, they celebrated their wedding anniversary *weekly*. Why wait a year when you have fifty-two opportunities? Since Ed and I met later in life—we were in our sixties—and, remembering Eileen's weekly ritual, I made it ours. Because we met on a Friday and had our first date on a Friday, we celebrate our good fortune every Friday. As I'm writing, we've celebrated 525 Fabulous Fridays, and counting.

By the time Babe was in her mid-nineties, "sharing fun is the whole thing," and "celebrate everything" became "never miss happy hour." At her senior residence, as happy hour approached, she'd often say, "Oh, I've got to get some pep. I don't know if I'll go tonight." But she always managed to get on the elevator and go downstairs to the pub for the camaraderie, for her two scotch and sodas, and for gathering around the campfire of community.

LESSON 7:

THE HAPPINESS OF GIVING *AND* RECEIVING FLOWERS

It was always easy to spot Dad in a crowd because he was the one who had a spring in his step. When he walked, he *bounced*! off the balls of his feet, and this was without the aid of springy, cushy-soled sport shoes—and never more so than when he was bounding into the house with flowers for his sweetheart. They were usually gladiolas. Since Gladys was Babe's given name, sometime early in their courtship the two of them must have adopted that long, spiky, colorful bloom as "their" flower. There were usually glads in the house, their romantic currency.

"So, Dad brought you gladiolas?" I said to Babe.

"He knew I liked them. It was as simple as that," she said. "And he brought them just anytime."

We'd been discussing her grandson Tony and the frustrating discussion we'd had on his recent visit to Southern California about his unwillingness to bring flowers to the woman who was the love of his life, the woman he was living with.

"Of course, it depends on the money," said Babe. "Tony isn't rich, but I feel the way Jade does."

The Jade Babe was identifying with had hair dyed pitch black, facial piercings, and, on her chest, a tattoo of an eagle whose wingtips extended up past her collarbone. But when it came to how this early-thirties, punk-looking woman, who'd been raised mostly in foster care, wanted to be treated by the special man in her life, tough-looking Jade was as much of a softie as Babe.

I explained to Mom how the four of us—Ed and I, Tony and Jade—had been hanging around the kitchen, making dinner, when the subject of a man bringing a woman flowers had come up. Tony had protested. "They're expensive," he said. "A hundred and twenty dollars a bouquet."

"On my way home from work, I get flowers at Trader Joe's," said Jade.

"Look at that bouquet there," said Tony, pointing to a slender vase of gorgeous white lilies on the kitchen counter.

"They were ten dollars at the farmers' market," I said. "Ten dollars. Total."

"What's the quid pro quo if I bring her flowers?" said Tony. "What do I get if I give her flowers?"

Ed and I exchanged a look of disbelief. Quid pro quo for *flowers*?

"Not every gesture has an equal market exchange," said Ed.

"You get the Tony dance," said Jade, who demonstrated a butt-wiggling, hip-gyrating, happy-you're-home jig.

I told Tony that in the beginning of our relationship Ed was tentative when he brought me flowers.

"Ed, timid?" said Tony, who was clearly unfamiliar with the shy side of his hotshot lawyer uncle.

I explained that Ed would come into the house, cradling one of those cellophane-wrapped, multicolored bouquets, the prearranged kind you can pick up at any grocery store, and he'd be nervous that it wouldn't please me, that I'd be critical. Instead of handing it to me directly, he'd keep the flowers close to his chest, an uncertain look on his face. Meanwhile, I was flattered that even at the grocery store that he'd dashed into to pick up some quick sushi for lunch, this man I loved had been thinking of *me*. Jade was nodding her head in agreement.

The three of us gave Tony a look that implied, *Buddy, it's so simple. Why don't you get it?*

Tony nodded. Maybe our message was hitting home after all.

By the way, I always wondered why Ed, of all people, such a self-confident individual, would be shy about bringing flowers home. It didn't compute until a daughter-in-law told me about Ed's late wife: how he'd brought her a bouquet and she'd complained because it contained carnations. *Carnations.* I told my daughter-in-law I'd be happy with whatever flowers my lover brought me.

Babe's lesson about the wisdom and romance of giving *and* receiving flowers has pretty much permeated the entire family, including Tony's father, my brother. The first time I visited his new home, front and center, presiding boldly on the glass table behind the couch, was a tall bouquet he'd just given his bride—orange gladiolas, exactly what Dad would have brought Mom.

LESSON 8:

THE *GOOD* GOODBYE

When my parents entertained, they would walk their guests out to their cars, tuck them in, and then, standing with their arms around each other, wave until the guests were well on their way, sending them off with a benediction, a *good* goodbye.

Described simply like this—arms around each other, happily waving—it doesn't seem to be all that much for anyone to emulate, to hold up as a behavioral yardstick, a lesson for a lifetime. And yet.

When Ed and I moved into the home where we're living now, it could have been tempting and it would have felt natural to begin and end the leave-taking with our guests at the front door. But remembering the warmth of my parents' goodbyes—how they softened the blow of the departure—we walk our guests down the front steps (there are only *three*) and watch and wave.

Standing out on the sidewalk, Ed has said, "Let's go back inside," and he's given me a kiss. Meanwhile, our guests are buckling themselves in, turning on the ignition. "I don't want to stay out here for no reason," he's said.

"No, we have to wait," I've explained.

The driver usually rolls down his or her window and waves back at us. Often I throw kisses, and sometimes our friends toot their horn. Our reward—or my reward, because by this point Ed's usually gone back inside—in the to and fro of this goodbye dance is that sometimes the guests also yell out another final "Love you!"

"It's necessary to keep *waving*?" asked my friend Linda, when we were discussing what I've come to think of as the "departing gesture."

I nodded. Although I'd never said it in so many words, yes, in my family it was necessary to keep waving.

I'd never thought about the "departing gesture" until I started noticing how other people give it such short shrift. Some hosts, even a particularly favorite one, remain seated in their living room, which prompts the departing guest (me) to mumble, "Oh, don't bother getting up. I'll see myself out." Even if it's dark out there and you end up stumbling around to find your car.

"The parting gesture expresses the sorrow that someone is leaving," said Linda. "It demonstrates, *Let's hang on to this experience; it was great.*" She paused. "Now you've made me think. With my son going off to college, we arranged a car for him, but did I walk him down and out to the car? Did he experience loneliness because I didn't do that?"

"That's different," I said. "That was New York City."

I was giving Linda a pass because she's a good friend and I love her, and it *was* New York City, and there can be so much rigmarole getting out of your apartment, down the elevator, and out to the street. But at the same time I was also struggling to understand this family ritual that I took for granted and I was still dragging around. Was it all that important, or could I drop it?

Parting and separating, leave-taking, isn't easy for me. Ed will come into my office and say goodbye, and kiss me while I'm at my desk. Yet when I hear the garage door open as he's about to leave, I'll always race downstairs and kiss him again. "I thought we already did that," he's been known to say.

Later in life, after Babe moved into a senior apartment, her friend Helene would stop in to play gin rummy and have lunch. The first time Helene departed, Amanda, Babe's caregiver, saw her to the door and assumed that was that.

"It's not nice to shut the door on people," said Babe. "They'll think we think, *Thank God they're leaving.*" Babe could no longer run after Helene, but she asked Amanda to open the door, see Helene down the hall, and wait with her at the elevator.

"Your Dad and I weren't perfect, but. . . ." Her voice trailed off.

As with many new immigrants, caregiving was Amanda's first job in America. (In Nicaragua, she'd received a degree in industrial design, and her husband reminded us that her diploma was handy in case any of us wanted to see it again.) Although Amanda was plenty smart, she was pretty slow picking up on Babe's art of the *good* goodbye.

Once, when I was leaving Houston after a visit, Babe offered to drive me to the airport. This meant that Amanda would drive me in Babe's car because Babe had stopped driving. It was a beautiful Sunday afternoon when we set off for George Bush Intercontinental Airport, freeway traffic was especially light, and, although driving someone to the airport isn't my idea of fun, in the front seats, Amanda and her copilot were as cheerful as little kids on a special outing.

"Snicklefritz really knows how to use that contraption," said Babe, pointing to the portable Garmin GPS Amanda had suctioned to the dash. (An aside: it was not lost on me how freely Babe gave compliments to Amanda, someone outside the family. See Lesson 11: Never Leave a Compliment Unsaid.)

When we arrived at the departure terminal, Amanda braked at the curb and popped open the trunk, all while she remained firmly buckled in the driver's seat. I got my bag out, but before Amanda could speed off, Mom insisted, "I have to say goodbye."

Although we'd already said goodbye, Amanda's businesslike send-off was too hasty for Babe. Her efficiency lacked a certain gracefulness and charm. And, for a change, this wasn't one of those crazy, jammed-up airport-traffic days, so there was no urgency for me to jump out fast and grab my roller bag before the airport police gave Amanda a talking-to.

Mom rolled down her window, and I opened her car door for another final kiss, a pat, and a wave. This extra petting, hand holding, and lingering signaled, *I'm sorry you're leaving. I'll miss you.*

"Come back anytime," she said. "I never tire of you." And then the final, motherly parting: "Behave yourself."

In 2013, Ed and I visited his son and his family in Connecticut, and we had what we thought was one of our best visits. When the taxi arrived, all seven of us—including three grandchildren—had congregated in the front hallway, spilling out onto the porch. We'd hugged and kissed and fussed and re-hugged and promised we'd get together again soon. Then Ed and I proceeded down the brick walkway to the car. Before

I got in, I glanced back toward the house. The front door was shut tight. Not one person was still throwing us a final goodbye kiss, a wave. It felt so lonely. In that stark, empty moment, I missed my parents more than I had almost anytime since I'd been an adult.

Although our eleven-year-old grandson had even declined a sleepover so he could be around to say goodbye to us in the morning, something was not right, and I felt it. I tried letting it drop, cutting them some slack, chalking it up to "different families do things differently." But I couldn't shake the nagging feeling that cold farewell transmitted.

That evening it still stung, and I was caught by surprise when the feeling spread to Ed: *Your family doesn't know how to say goodbye, so I'm not making love with you.* Poor Ed.

Was it boorish of me to interpret that goodbye so negatively? Maybe we Gieses cleave and cling too long? It turned out I'd caught the vibe correctly. Slowly, it dribbled out that Ed's son and his wife were disappointed with us; they felt we hadn't paid enough attention to their eldest child. We'd started taking the six grandchildren on individual adventures—whale watching in Baja, hiking in Big Sur—and hadn't yet stepped up to invite their eldest son, who was twelve and autistic. Quickly, we made amends and asked James, who had never traveled away from his parents, to choose a city. He picked Washington, DC, because Ed had lived there, and he elected to travel by train. Because James had a fascination with the presidents (he'd already memorized all their birth dates), for three days we toured presidential monuments, ate french fries at lunch and dinner, visited Ed's old house in Bethesda, and somehow, even in Washington, DC, managed to avoid the triggers his parents had warned us set him off: crowds, lines, and traffic.

After we returned James safely home, their goodbye was fabulously warm. The entire family stayed out on the porch, lingering and waving—pretty much exactly the way my family would have done it.

LESSON 9:

PEOPLE DON'T LIKE TO BE AROUND DEPRESSED PEOPLE

In my parents' bedroom, there was a large, framed poster of a boy and a girl holding hands, with the caption "I can't make it alone." This was at a time when dependency had gone out of style, and, as someone who viewed herself as an independent feminist, I found that poster offensive. *What do you mean, Babe? Of course you can make it alone!* (Probably that poster rattled me so much because it touched a personal nerve. I was still in denial that if something happened in my marriage, I wouldn't *want* to make it alone.)

My parents had been married almost fifty-four years when my father died. I had reason to worry that Babe, eighty-one and alone for the first time in her adult life, would be lost, adrift, depressed. *I can't make it alone.* Haven't we all heard about "broken-heart syndrome," when a long-married spouse dies and the surviving spouse follows soon afterward?

Instead, while my father's ashes were still warm, Babe renewed her passport. From the crematorium, where we chose a plain cardboard cylinder (because Babe knew Dad wouldn't want her wasting good money on anything fancy), my sister and I took Babe directly to the passport office in downtown Seattle.

In keeping with Dad's spirit, instead of a funeral or a memorial, we hosted a party in their condo. By the front door, we stacked up dozens of his jumpsuits, and, wearing a baby-blue one, I handed them out as party favors when friends departed. Then Babe left the country with my sister and her husband and a dozen of their friends on a trip to France that had been planned beforehand; at the last minute, my sister had insisted on adding Babe. I worried that it was too soon, that she'd be crying all the way from Paris to Strasbourg. Instead, it was just right.

"Life is for the living!" Babe said, as I helped her pack her sturdy blue Samsonite luggage.

She probably wasn't familiar with the term *carpe diem*, but at critical times during tragic transitions— when her mother died, when her husband died—she embodied it in bold, blazing colors. Life is for the living.

When times got even tougher, when Babe had out-lived not only Dad but all their friends, and even when her only remaining sister, Aunt Dell, died, Babe's behavior, which I'd describe as almost upbeat, puzzled me.

"Why aren't you depressed?" I asked her.

"People don't like to be around depressed people," she said.

Oh.

For Babe, who was sociable, it was that simple. Dealing with loss required an attitude adjustment. She *chose* not to sink into despair because she didn't want to be a social outcast.

I mistrusted that it could be so easy. All those years and years I'd spent in therapy, could I have done it Babe's way? No way. Not yet. Back then, I was still too confused, too young, too immature.

It wasn't always that easy for Babe, either. She'd had to grow into this maturity. Way back when she was a young mother of two, when her mother came to live with us, when her dashing husband was away on business too often, in eight years she suffered *five* heartbreaking miscarriages. Coming from a family of four sisters, she'd desperately wanted more children, five children, which had made me think, *What's wrong with who's already here? Aren't my brother and me enough?* To say she sunk into a valley of depression is an understatement.

My parents had always had an easy physical relationship. I liked how Babe sat on my father's lap with her arms around his neck. So when I hadn't seen much physical affection between them, I asked her about it. She said, "We don't have that same chair in the kitchen anymore."

Oh.

As a self-centered preteen and adolescent, I never discussed with Babe what had lifted her depression. I know she never saw a therapist—cognitive or otherwise. But I also know research indicates that genes strongly influence a propensity toward optimism. It's likely that Babe was genetically predisposed to seeing the glass half-full, or more, and had been thrown off by those sad years of miscarriages.

In my twenties, I probably spent—wasted?—too much time in therapy discussing my mother's depression and how it weighed me down. Poor me. That was the 1970s in New York City, where everyone in certain circles on the Upper West Side of Manhattan seemed to have a therapist. I would come to understand that Babe's was a situational depression—all those miserable miscarriages. Years later, I suffered through a similar situational depression because of infertility and a miserable first marriage.

Later in life, Babe had evolved. I looked around: Where was the depressed mother I'd spent so much time complaining about in therapy? Babe had outgrown the mental mom I carried with me, and it had taken me a while to catch up.

Around 2012, when communications with my siblings threatened to break down, I considered returning to therapy. Instead, having grown into being Babe's daughter, I adopted a personal mantra: *In spite of what's happening, it's okay to be happy today.* Because if I let myself wallow in unhappiness, sink into sadness, descend into depression, then I wouldn't be any good to anyone—to Ed, my family, my friends, myself. *People don't like to be around depressed people.*

This is decidedly not a superficial, tacked-on, Pollyanna happiness, the happy-happy face of a Hallmark card. This is a deep, hard-earned connection with the vividly positive, instead of the bleakly negative. It reminds me of a quote, attributed to Abraham Lincoln, that is boldly painted on an entire side of a building on Lincoln Boulevard in West LA: "Most folks are about as happy as they make up their minds to be." Babe couldn't have said it better.

I've passed my mantra on and on and on. When a grandson was teased at summer camp to the point where he packed up and left, I suggested he try my mantra. When a very best friend fell into despair over a financial situation and was torn apart by the prospect of being forced to sue her son, I suggested she try my mantra. When another friend kept delaying a trip home because her mentally ill brother had violently shoved her mother, and both of them had ended up hospitalized, I suggested she get her plane ticket and try my mantra. *In spite of what's happening, it's okay to be happy today.*

Babe would have approved.

LESSON 10:

DON'T BE DRAB

In March 2011, I left LAX on an early flight to make sure I arrived at Babe's new place in Houston in time for dinner at five o'clock. As I entered her apartment, the first words out of her mouth were, "You're wearing *that*? You used to wear such colorful clothes. You look drab."

"Mom, gimme a break. I just got off the plane!"

I was joining her new friends for the first time in the senior community she'd just moved into, and I'd forgotten that she'd want to show me off. My travel outfit—comfortable black exercise pants, black work-out shirt, clunky gym shoes—was, as she would have put it, nothing to write home about.

"Don't be drab" was one of Babe's central mantras.

Babe was the anti-Eileen Fisher. Always.

For decades, the fashion industry has written an obituary for color. You know the stores where every rack features the dominant "colors" of regulation black and ash gray? I don't even bother to poke my head in those places, where it's so grim and gloomy it looks like someone died. A black-dressing friend confided, "My daughter says my husband and I dress like communists."

After Coco Chanel's lover died in 1919, she began wearing black, and thus was born the little black dress. But the little black dress was created because someone *died*. Ever since then, women have worn this grim garment as if it's cocktail chic and not Coco Chanel's widow's weeds.

In contrast, Babe asserted herself through happy bursts of bold color. When she was thirty-nine and pregnant (finally) with my sister, she wore a ruby-red maternity dress. Its knife-edge pleats flared from a floppy bow at the neckline all the way to the hem. I was nine, and I've never forgotten when she leaned over the flowing crimson cascade. If ever there was a power dress, that was it: it was colorful, fashionable, and glamorous. Like Babe. Did she also favor red because she knew the color had an extra "pop" against the gray, cloudy skies of Seattle? Maybe.

She practiced color therapy long before fashionistas codified it, and she never needed to hire a color consultant to determine her palette. She knew color broadcasted how she felt and made her attractive—in that color *attracted* people to her. She wasn't narcissistic. It wasn't, *Look at me, how gorgeous I am*. Whether she was with the amiable husband-and-wife managers at the corner grocery store who cashed her checks or with a next-door neighbor, it was more, *Look at me, I'm accessible and fun. Let's be friends*. She knew that a splash of color added a dose of happiness to herself and others.

Wearing color was about more than looking pretty, though Babe certainly favored that, too. (Babe's beauty guidelines included: book beauty appointments; wear makeup; and whatever you do, don't go gray. Gray isn't necessary. It just shows your age.) For Babe, wearing color was about being part of the social conversation, being *engaged* with others.

I had a memorable experience with the power of color to attract when I was visiting the Taj Mahal and happened to be wearing a saffron-colored kurta with matching cotton pants. I was there at sunrise, the perfect time to experience that immense seventeenth-century white marble mausoleum bathed in dawn's early glow. Many Indian visitors, because the Taj is also one of their favorite pilgrimage sites, kept bowing to me. "You're a healer," they'd say, their hands folded in prayer. *To me. The Holy Me.* I kept shaking my head no. But my plain saffron outfit, which I'd bought for something like ten dollars at a gas station where our UCLA tour bus had stopped, was the same saffron color of the robes that the Hindu holy men wore. The golden color positively glowed, and maybe I did, too—that trip to India was the first time I'd felt happy since my husband's death. Finally I realized, *If it makes these people happy for a blond, pigtailed traveler from LA to be a holy person, okay.* From then on, when the Indian men in their white cotton kurtas and the women in their dazzling saris bowed to me—to the holy, life-giving color I was wearing—I folded my hands in prayer, murmured, *"Namaste,"* the only Indian word I knew, and bowed back.

When I was young, Babe dressed us in matching mother-daughter outfits, often ones like the red-and-white-plaid wool suit she'd sewn on her Singer sewing machine, which she operated with a foot pump. Mine had a tiny bolero vest with a pleated miniskirt. (What else could it be but a mini, when I was only so high?) Because of the many photos showing me happily wearing that outfit, smiling so broadly my face squinted, I also know that Babe paired it with Mary Janes and white socks that had a ruffled lace edge. When I was about ten, I rebelled and wouldn't be caught dead in any of her outfits. A white cotton blouse with a ruffled collar, no way; for me, a starched, tailored shirt with cuff links I'd borrowed from my dad.

After moving far away from home and recoiling at the thought that I was anything like my mother—*I'm a journalist in New York City*!—I was struck dumb one day when I looked in my closet and realized how thoroughly I'd become my mother's daughter. The sea change had happened so slowly that by my fifties, her clothes were exactly what I liked. From what depths had she managed to creep so completely back into my psyche—though probably she'd never left—and my closet? An admission: no matter how much I thought I was rebelling, even during those times when I lived far away—first New York City and then LA—I still went home for every holiday, and never empty-handed.

According to a poll conducted by the British website Dotty Bingo, by age thirty-one, daughters start to resemble their mothers. I must have been slow, because for me it was decades later. However, by my fifties, my closet was filled with what were essentially mother-daughter outfits. Again. But now I gratefully inherited her hand-me-downs. Hers weren't designer outfits, but, trust me, these were not little-old-lady items, either: a black Chinese jacket with a fabulous red-and-gold silk lining, a fancy white sweater vest encrusted with pearls, an orange jacket with the sunniest marigold lining. Even her colors—turquoise, pinks, reds—had become my favorites.

The beauty of learning a lesson and incorporating it so fully that it becomes part of you, as if it were your original chromosomal material, is that you can casually pass it on without even noticing.

On my first date with Ed, after he rang the bell but before I opened the door, I peeked out the peephole and saw a man wearing the dullest beige plaid flannel shirt. (Flannel in August in Southern California?) Although Ed was a lean, lanky six foot three, that limp sad sack of a shirt accurately reflected how he felt: his wife had died fourteen months earlier, after forty-one years of marriage, and I was his first date. After thirty-eight years of practicing law in Washington, DC, he'd made a fresh break to the West Coast to teach at the law school at Pepperdine. We'd been introduced by a mutual friend, Alice Starr.

Alice hadn't mentioned that Ed Warren was from Kentucky. I've always been a sucker for a super-smart man with a charming Southern drawl, the kind of down-home accent that cleverly camouflages the fact that his impressive office in Washington, DC, overlooked the White House. On our second date, after we'd gone hiking, attended what Ed referred to as a "hippie party" up in the hills, and lain side by side on the double-wide turquoise chaise lounge on my deck, and after he'd responded tremulously to my touch—I'd never felt a man *tremble* when I touched him—and after we'd talked about marriage and our getting married (yes, this on our second date), he asked if I'd help him shop for some clothes. In no time, he shoved aside his Kirkland & Ellis suits (they were in my closet already—we married nine months after we met) and in their place hung linen shirts in a rainbow of sensual colors—mango, pumpkin, ocean blue, rooster red. With his tanned skin, he looked gorgeous in these vibrant tones. Even his Patagonia hiking shirts were now salmon and turquoise.

Ever since I took Babe's "don't be drab" lesson to heart, the experience of radiating color, *becoming* color, happens often, sometimes in the weirdest of circumstances. One morning, a year or so after we met, Ed was scheduled for a colonoscopy, and, after he'd had a miserable night of preparation, I woke up early to drive him to the endoscopy center. To cheer myself up—because, let's face it, this is a procedure that none of us looks forward to, right?—I reached for the orange jacket with a mandarin collar that I'd just inherited from Mom. It has the sunniest silk lining of fluorescent marigolds, which burst out when the cuffs are turned up.

At the endoscopy center, Ed had changed into a hospital gown and was in bed, swaddled in layers of warmed blankets. I was sitting on a chair next to him when a woman in scrubs and a shower cap padded in and introduced herself as his anesthesiologist. But, before glancing at Ed's chart, she turned to me. "I *love* that color!" she said. In that dimly lit, hushed, antiseptic gray, shiveringly cold pre-op holding area, I was my own little blaze of marigolds. "You've made my day!" she said.

Another time, I was scheduled for spinal surgery for a neck so stiff that I couldn't turn my head when I was driving. After my internist nixed the surgery as too aggressive for my symptoms, I plunged into a rehab program, and that's when I met Lana, a massage worker from Croatia. But to call her a massage worker is to do her an injustice, because it felt as though she was realigning all my internal organs, not just the two bulging discs, C3 and C4, in my neck. However, every time this forty-three-year-old woman—who spoke five languages and who had escaped Sarajevo on the last plane when the Bosnian civil war broke out in 1992—showed up with her table, she was wearing frumpy black sweats. She was so anti-Babe I couldn't stand it. (She looked pretty much like I had that time I showed up at Babe's for dinner in travel black.)

This was at a time when my neck was so rigid that when I woke up in the morning, it felt as though it was going to break off. When you're hurting that much, if you trust someone enough to let them touch that most fragile part of your body, let alone knead it deeply and stretch it, you can form a bond pretty quickly. Because of that intimate connection, during one of my treatments I explained Babe's "don't be drab" philosophy and commented to Lana that she always showed up looking so funereal that it depressed me.

"I'm afraid of being too noticeable," she said. Her features—shiny black curls, pale skin, a curious expression—were those of an attractive, intelligent individual who was hiding behind a shroud. She explained that, especially for work, she had a uniform: black or gray clothes. "I let my work speak for itself," she said. "I thought I'd be taken more seriously as a student, a worker, an employee."

At my suggestion, Lana added color: a plum T-shirt. It was such a muddy tone it might as well have been black.

"In my mind, it looks like red," she said.

It's true that someone doing work as intimate as massage shouldn't wear salacious clothing. But I wasn't urging her to tart up her look by baring cleavage; I was only suggesting a color other than black. For Christmas I gave her a not-drab red tank top. I suggested she wear it over her black uniform; she wore it under her work clothes. She said it was such a difficult shift to add color that it would have been easier to be naked.

Unbeknownst to me, I had an ally halfway around the world. When Lana went home to Mostar, Croatia, her father couldn't stand seeing his gorgeous only daughter, who'd been adventurous enough to leave for America and to end up in the sunshine state, schlepping around in her somber uniforms. He insisted that while she was in his house she wear one of his T-shirts, which happened to be red.

When Lana told me about her dad, I'd just bought myself a new red T-shirt. I gave it to her with the price tag still attached. "But unless you're going to wear it," I said, "don't take it."

Lana had helped rehab my neck, and for her that lipstick red T-shirt was the catalyst for her rehab. She told me what happened next: "The first time I wore your shirt, I wore it to the beach with my girlfriend—just your red shirt and jeans—and she said, 'Wow, look at you! You're all dressed up.' When you got me started,

I noticed more red—a bowl of strawberries, the red moon, stop signs, fire trucks, the red on Colgate toothpaste. The world is not black and white. It's colorful." By then Lana had also graduated to faded red cargo pants. "If only we could bottle this and share it with everyone," she said.

Babe, at ninety-six, still dressed to the nines, with jewelry to match. That Easter she asked me, "Did you get a new outfit?"

I'd forgotten.

Henry David Thoreau said, "Beware of all enterprises that require new clothes." Maybe. But Thoreau didn't know Babe.

LESSON 11:

NEVER LEAVE A COMPLIMENT UNSAID

Sometimes Mother doesn't know best. I learned a few life lessons the messy way—by doing the opposite of what Babe did.

By now you know that Babe had a lot of admirable talents and social graces, but giving praise, at least to me, her eldest daughter, wasn't one of them. Mind you, she liked getting compliments herself; as she said, "They kind of build you up a bit."

In 1961, while competing in the Sam Houston High School Speech and Debate Tournament, I won five First Places in Drama, Improvisation, Debate,

Poetry, and even Bible. (This was Texas, after all.) At home, I was probably beaming as brightly as my armload of trophies.

"Don't be conceited," Babe said.

Conceited? I was concentrating too hard on lining up all the trophies and medals single file across the front edge of our Motorola black-and-white TV console to feel wounded.

"It goes to your head, and it isn't fun," she said. "You know, *I* ironed the blouse you wore."

She ironed the blouse I wore. But I *earned* those First Places. This was back in the day when a trophy still meant something. Way before the era when everyone gets one for showing up. That citywide tournament in Houston had attracted hundreds of competitors, and most had gone home empty-handed. And discovering a talent for public speaking held a special sweetness for someone who had started talking late.

In the first grade, it was determined that I had a speech impediment. During Mrs. Peffley's class, instead of reading *Dick and Jane* along with the other kids, I was sent out of class, up the creaky wooden stairs, to the second floor of Whitworth Elementary, to meet with the speech therapist. Later, when I stumbled accidentally upon an audio recording from that time, it seemed clear that my "problem" was that I was so enthusiastic and excited, so *amped* about telling stories, that my words tumbled out on top of each other, smashing into each other, so no one could understand the "jabberwocky" that rushed out. What was also impressive about that old recording was that the little girl sounded like the happiest kid: she was bubbling over, *oozing* delight. She didn't have a lisp or a stutter or any other speech *impediment*. Little Jo Ann just needed to slow down, like Mrs. Peffley had written in my report card.

Now, wouldn't most parents go out of their way to praise, maybe even brag, about a child whose speech was once unintelligible, who was also a nervous nail biter, but who overcame that early handicap to win prizes in public speaking?

When Ed, who adored Babe, and I discussed why someone would withhold praise, Ed explained it this way: "When you won all those trophies, your mom wanted credit for her contribution. Otherwise, she felt diminished."

As a child, I didn't understand a whiff of this, but now it brings to mind a mother-daughter passage from Allan Gurganus's novella *Saints Have Mothers*. The teenage daughter says to her mother, "Admit you think I'm an overachiever . . . But why must you almost make that mean you're *under*achieving? I'm just in *high school*."

Does this help explain the dynamic that existed between my mother and me? Maybe. Or was it more that Babe was a product of her generation? Was hers a 1950's style of parenting: don't brag about your child; be modest?

I do know Babe *said* she didn't compliment her children because she didn't want to play favorites. But, as an incredulous friend suggested, "She could have given compliments to all three of you!" Exactly.

Today, even the manufacturers of those fitness-tracker wristbands understand that they may nag us at intervals throughout the day, but to be user-friendly they also have to hand out praise. And it seems to work—even if it is prerecorded, digital praise from an inanimate device.

Since I know how good it feels to receive a compliment—not just from a fitness band, and even in a somewhat compromising situation. Once during a gynecology exam, I'd scooted all the way down to the end of the table, my feet were in the stirrups, and one of those crinkly modesty sheets had been spread over my private area. The doctor had started the pelvic exam, never the most pleasant experience, and she said, "You have strong abdominal muscles. Really strong."

Afterward, I went to Gold's Gym, in Venice, for my workout, and, buoyed by that praise—*I'm really strong!*—I floated from machine to machine, even the cranky ones that I usually don't like. I couldn't help but notice the powerfully buoyant effect of those two sentences—only two sentences, but positive ones.

Did Babe's behavior make me more needy for compliments?

Probably.

Did that make me more generous in giving out compliments?

Definitely.

Because I know how it hurts not to receive a positive comment, I've adopted a different behavior: I try never to let a compliment go unsaid. If I ever *think* something positive about someone or something—even the most fleeting thought—I share it before it vanishes. Perhaps it's my decades of meditation training that have led me to fear I'll be harmed if I keep the positive idea unspoken—if I withhold it, hoard it, and don't share it.

I guess this could backfire, but I can't recall that ever happening. The young coffee barista might have mistakenly thought I was hitting on him when I complimented him on his cool plaid tie. Instead, he tossed one my way and said he liked my "Harry Potter glasses." A virtuous circle. For that mini-moment, hardly calculable, we smiled at each other and basked in a small space of social sweetness.

Or take the time I was placing an order with a florist. The woman I was speaking with seemed thrilled I'd called. And mine wasn't some big order that would save the day—just a little arrangement for my friend Nanette's birthday. It turned out that I was speaking with the owner, and before I hung up, I told her she had the best phone personality, which she did.

"You just made my week," she said.

Her *week*? That such a simple comment made by a total stranger had struck such a chord made me wonder what difficulties she was going through. Because most of the time, we don't have a clue about the struggles other people are up against, and yet a social nicety, a mini-compliment out of the blue—though it must be an authentic one; it can't be insincere or something phony, trumped up for social lubrication—has the power to touch people profoundly.

Another time, I was at a store, and as the clerk was ringing up the sale, I glanced at the woman standing next to me in line. She was a plump, middle-age brunette wearing a sundress made out of a crisp cotton piqué. I complimented her on her yellow dress, how cheerful and summery it was. I said yellow was one of my favorite colors, and I pointed to my sunshine-yellow purse.

"Thank you so much for saying that," she said, barely holding back tears. "You don't know how much that means to me. I just came from a funeral, and everyone was wearing black. People told me I was being disrespectful. But I thought the deceased—a friend in his eighties—would appreciate something cheerful."

I'd just shared another spur-of-the-moment reaction—this time to the happy color of someone's dress—and I wasn't expecting such an outpouring. I had no idea I was giving a gift to someone who needed one so deeply. She took my comment as an affirmation of her very self—regardless of what her girlfriends had said, she wasn't a bad person for having worn a sunny color to a funeral. She was okay. And isn't that what we all crave? To feel we're okay?

After that brief encounter, I walked away with an extra bounce in my step, and probably she did, too. Giving a compliment releases energy and relaxes the spirit. Besides, it's fun. It adds an extra punctuation mark, a *spark*!, and life feels momentarily fuller. And giving a compliment is such an easy, fluent currency.

I was listening once as Ed, who is not a touchy-feely kind of guy, explained this positive "force field" concept to our hardest-to-please, then-eleven-year-old grandchild, the one who had an uncanny ability to ferret out and emphasize the negative in every situation. "It's a positive energy, a receptivity, an openness," he said. "Because Jo gives out compliments so freely, she's also the recipient of constant compliments. And it's not from the same people, either."

When Babe was ninety-five, to celebrate New Years Eve, my brother and his wife, Lynn, drove Babe and Ellen, her caregiver at the time, from Houston to Bozeman, Montana, where Ed and I have a home. ("Never turn down a road trip" was another of Babe's maxims.) All of us wanted to celebrate New Years together in snowy Montana, and we agreed that at ninety-five, Babe shouldn't fly in winter. What if a snowstorm delayed her flight? She still had the stamina for a direct three-hour flight, but not for a layover in a strange city while a storm passed. So my brother, who likes to drive long distances, and Babe, who loved to be driven, set off from Houston.

Three days later, the happy foursome arrived in high spirits. As they walked down the freshly salted and plowed walkway, with snow still falling, and burst inside, I got such a kick out of seeing Babe and Jimmy together—the real Mutt and Jeff: Jimmy was nearly seven feet tall, while Babe, gripping her walker, was down to five feet plus an inch or two.

The next day, Babe was sitting inside, cozy, by the warmth of a crackling fire. Looking out over snowy Bridger Canyon, which opened below us like a vast white inland sea, she asked if we were at the top of the mountain. I explained that we were only about three-quarters of the way up: we were at 5,500 feet, and the top was about 7,000 feet.

Our unpaved rural road was usually two lanes of washboard-bumpy gravel, but by late December it was reduced to one snow-plowed lane, if we were lucky. The afternoon of New Year's Eve Day, it had stopped snowing, and the sun was sparkling diamonds on the fresh snow. Since cabin fever had settled in, I decided it was time for us to get some fresh air. I'd drive us all the way up our mountain to that special place that makes you feel like you're on top of the whole world and the snowcapped, big-sky vista stretches in every direction.

Babe, Ellen, and I piled into Ed's sturdy 1998 blue Tahoe, which looks like a tank and drives like a truck, which is a good thing when you live in the country. For our little joyride, Babe was belted into the passenger seat, and Ellen was in the middle of the back. As we started off, the tires crunched into a fresh layer of powdery snow—perfect, easy driving conditions. The uphill shoulder was lined with a stand of evergreens so pretty they looked like a row of Christmas trees.

Winter owned that dazzling, golden afternoon. Before the first curve, on the sloping hillside over on the next mountain, we spotted a herd of about a hundred elk grazing shoulder to shoulder. Their glossy auburn coats were as lustrous as if they'd been rinsed with hair conditioner. Such an abundance of healthy wildlife—elk, moose, deer—and often just outside our kitchen window, is what makes winter in Montana so breathtaking.

At the third turn, this one a steep, hairpin curve, the tires on the Tahoe started spinning. In spite of our four-wheel drive and snow tires, the wheels began sliding sideways to the right. There was no guard rail, no shoulder; in a foot or so, we'd be slipping off the road, tumbling down the mountain.

In that winter white radiance, the sun glared on all sides, except on that icy patch in the shade. I squinted for a safe place to turn around. The road had frozen to a sheet of black ice, and we were stranded, skidding, in the middle of it.

What do I do now? Abandon the car? Start walking? But there was no way Babe could walk down the mountain, even if we hadn't left her walker behind in the garage. Lord knows what Ellen, who was from the Philippines and had never seen snow, thought about our dangerous predicament.

That was when I had the awful realization that I had no choice but to reverse down the mountain. I'm a fair-weather driver who learned to drive in Texas, and driving backward on black ice exceeds my expertise.

But before the car slid to the side and we fell off the mountain, I cranked it in reverse. I opened my window to cool off and, focusing on the rearview mirror, inched us down. I'd gone a hundred yards or so, and backed us off the iciest patch, when I started breathing again.

That's when Babe said, "You're such a good driver, Jo Ann!"

Her comment registered profoundly because it was one of the rare, straight-out compliments Babe ever gave me. It took that much fear to prompt a compliment out of her (and for her to resort to my baby name).

During the last year I visited Babe, she was in her living room, sitting in front of the fireplace, where the mantel was crowded with Hummel figurines. Although it was summer in Houston and sweltering outside, Babe was wearing long underwear under her outfit, and I'd also just handed her a thick wool poncho-style shawl. The room thermostat was set at ninety, and the gas logs were switched on high for even more heat. Sometimes, if I thought she wasn't looking, I'd turn it off to give myself a break, but not this time.

I was sitting directly in front of her, almost knee to knee, to give her the best chance of hearing me, either through her hearing aids or by reading my lips.

"How long are you going to let your hair grow?" she asked.

"Probably down to my waist." I knew where this conversation was headed. This was in the same vein as when we used to play Scrabble and she'd look up from her tray of tiles, frown, and ask, "Since when did you stop wearing makeup? You used to look so pretty with blush and mascara." A year ago it was makeup; today, hair. My friend Pamela had recently commented that my thick, shoulder-length hair (the good-hair gene another inheritance from Babe) had never looked better.

"I prefer short hair," said Babe. A Clairol strawberry-blonde, she still had twice-weekly appointments with Able, who, down on the second floor, coiffed her thick hair in tight curls, which she insisted made her look younger. "Able just cut mine another two inches," she said.

"Josie's hair is beautiful!" my husband piped up from the far corner, where he was reading the *Houston Chronicle*. Bless Ed.

On weekends, my brother usually brought Babe a box of freshly baked sticky cinnamon buns. They were so large that her caregiver divided them into quarters. While I was at Central Market, restocking Babe's supply of fresh berries and ice cream sandwiches, I spied small cinnamon rugelachs in the bakery. I sampled one, and it tasted as heavenly as the sweets my grandmother used to bake. I also thought their miniature size—only two inches long—was a perfect Babe size.

"Well?" I asked, as she took her first bite.

"I've tasted better," she said.

See?

Now you understand why I always strive to speak to the positive. Another huge life lesson learned from Babe.

LESSON 12:

GO! WHILE YOU CAN

At ninety-five, Babe still had a valid US passport. But by then the most she could manage was a road trip to Montana, or a domestic flight from Houston to Los Angeles to visit me, and even that was a stretch. So I dreaded dropping the news that Ed and I were leaving for China. It didn't seem fair that I could still up and go and she couldn't.

I expected her to object—to complain that a month was too long, China was too far. Instead she said, "*Go!* while you can."

Go?

She told me about Dr. Wendell, who had delivered her three babies and had wanted to travel. By the time he was ready to retire, his wife was in a wheelchair.

"*Go!*" she said, bestowing a mother's blessing. "My travel days are getting shorter. I know that. I can't go as far, as often. Gosh, Bessie and I'd be together, and she'd say, 'Let's go to Canada!' and away we'd go. I can't do that anymore."

Babe had been my accomplice on many adventures. When I got an assignment to write a travel story about the San Juan Islands, she was my sidekick as we grilled fresh oysters at an oyster farm on Orcas Island. All I needed to do was say the word. An expedition to look at quilts in the Amish country, or lunch with my friends at Windows on the World, the restaurant on top of the World Trade Center (before it was destroyed by terrorists), and Babe was game. She asserted none of the scrutiny most companions would have insisted on—when, where, how long will we be gone? Babe's go-with-the-flow attitude was the opposite of a nervous, uptight, easily flustered traveler. The only time I remember her objecting to any arrangement I made was in Pennsylvania, at a nineteenth-century inn. She did not appreciate it when the clerk indicated that the shared toilet was way down at the far end of a public hall.

Once, after I returned from India, I couldn't stop raving about the Pushkar Camel Fair in Rajasthan and the Taj Lake Palace in Udaipur. Fingering the saffron kurta with gold threads that I'd brought her, Babe said wistfully, "It's too bad we didn't know earlier how much you'd love India"—meaning, we could have gone together.

Babe, who loved her home but wasn't a homebody, had always practiced "*Go!* while you can."

At first, travel had meant those modest road trips up and down the West Coast where Dad went inside for a business meeting while she embroidered outside in the car. Later, with my brother and me tagging along, family travel meant piling in Dad's Studebaker Golden Hawk and setting off from Seattle for some simple destination like Seaside or Roseburg, Oregon. While Dad drove, Babe, the navigator, flipped through one of those spiral-bound TripTiks from AAA. The quirky red-and-white Burma-Shave road signs posted along the edges of the highway—COVERS A MULTITUDE OF CHINS—passed for entertainment. When it got close to nightfall, my brother and I would pester our parents to pull over at any motel that AAA claimed had a swimming pool. Once, in Sun Valley (this was before it was *Sun Valley*), we swam in a steaming-hot pool with snowflakes falling on our shoulders.

When air travel became a possibility—remember Pan Am?—Babe wore a gabardine suit that was nipped in at the waist, the kind of ultra-shapely, feminine suit you rarely see these days, sling-back pumps with an open toe, and a hat with a half veil (the original retro look) that dipped just so over her forehead. Even if roller bags had existed, Babe wouldn't have been caught dead dragging one.

Eventually, my father's business became successful enough that he and Babe were able to take business trips to Norway, Taiwan, and Singapore. In Hong Kong they bought an ornately carved green "jade" urn. Somehow my sister got the idea that it would be our parents' funeral urn. Wendy inserted a divider—a piece of stiff cardboard from the dry cleaners—and on one side she had Dad write "Dad," in his scratchy, sixth-grade handwriting, and on the other side Mom wrote "Mom" in her graceful Palmer cursive.

And remember how Babe took her own advice to *Go!* While Dad's ashes were still warm (he hadn't even made it to the urn yet), she renewed her passport and up and left with my sister for France. And after her own mother died, she bought herself that cool red convertible.

I'd felt suffocated in the Studebaker zooming past potato fields in Idaho when I longed to see Paris. To make up for lost time, in my twenties I traveled with a vengeance. Like an addict who had overdosed on *National Geographic*s, I finagled trips—student travel and business trips—to Chile, Tokyo, East Berlin. I *needed* to see the Hong Kong Harbor before it deteriorated into just another industrial port and the taipans with their glorious red sails disappeared. I *had* to experience Margaret Mead's Bali before it morphed into a glitzy, garbage-littered tourist destination.

Mine were no idle, ho-hum, one-day-I'll-see-Paris daydreams; mine was a full-blown, passionate, not-to-be-denied *hunger*.

I was so amped to experience the world that sometimes I charged out on cheap student tickets, too fast, too alone, with no rip cord to pull. One morning I was waiting anxiously by the phone in my dingy hotel room in Bogota for my friend to tell me when she'd be picking me up. Marcella was a native of Colombia, and during our many lunches at the *Houston Post*—she was in the art department, I was a reporter—we'd planned to meet in Bogota and stay at her family's hacienda. When the phone finally rang, Marcella explained that they'd had a problem—the foreman at the hacienda had been beheaded (this was Colombia in the late '60s)—and she had to cancel our plans. When I hung up the phone in that dreary hotel room, I felt sick—sick for the foreman and the horror of his beheading, sick for Marcella and her family, but probably sickest for my own sorry self, a single traveler who was now stranded in a strange city. What was I supposed to do in that gray, rainy place where I didn't know anyone?

To shake off the disappointment and loneliness, I ventured out in search of a place to get my nails done. This wasn't a bimbo move. I didn't need some glossy mani. What I craved was warm contact with a motherly woman who would lessen the panic that so often accompanied my youthful adventures. At the time, I didn't realize that in seeking to get my nails done—to hold hands with an older woman to calm myself down, to be babied—I was reconnecting with (or regressing to) the primal security and comfort my grandmother had offered me.

Babe's mother, my grandmother Josie, had been my best friend. From the fifth year of my life until she went into a nursing home when I was twelve, we shared a bedroom, a closet, a dresser, and a lifetime. Josie was a woman of the nineteenth century whose stern wedding photo showed her dressed from head to toe in acres of white Victorian lace. She was the sort of grandmother who tended a row of African violets in saucers on the kitchen windowsill, who wore an apron, and who'd been a professional baker in Chicago. (Because my parents thought it was a disadvantage that I had to share a room with my grandmother, they compensated me by giving us the best room, the one that overlooked Lake Washington. Only there was no hardship—I had my grandmother *and* the lake!) Although by then we were a family of five, I knew that her gooey chocolate pudding pie, sticky cinnamon buns, lemon pies decorated with the prettiest peaks of swirling meringue, and German breakfast pancakes as thin as French crêpes were made especially for me. In return, I gave her manicures. I wasn't steady with the clippers, but I loved doing her nails because it meant I could hold her soft hands as long as I wanted.

When I told Babe that Ed and I would be leaving for China, I mentioned that on the way home we'd stop in Singapore.

"Your dad and I loved Singapore," Babe said. "Your dad wanted to retire there."

He did? That was the first I'd heard of it. While Babe reminisced about Singapore, I schemed how to include her on our trip.

For many, a longed-for bonus of travel is the chance to unplug, disconnect, a digital detox from office and family. But when you have a mother who was once a traveler and who is still curious about the world, you discover that if you want to, it's easy to stay connected.

The first misty morning at the Mutianyu section of the Great Wall, Ed and I arrived so early we were almost the only people clambering up the steep, uneven stone steps. On the drive back to Beijing, the pumpkins and cornhusks piled at roadside stands looked pretty much like the autumn farm stands back home. But the evening street food in Beijing—raw embryos, crickets, and grasshoppers—didn't look like anything back home. I downloaded the photos and sent them to Amanda, Babe's caregiver. First thing the next morning, I called Babe, who in Houston was a day behind, enjoying her first scotch and soda of the evening. Amanda pulled up a chair for Babe in front of the computer screen.

"I feel like I'm on the trip with you!" Babe said. Babe, the ninety-five year old postmodern, digital armchair traveler.

I felt the same way. When I spotted the pair of petrified walnuts that Mark Ma, our guide, had inherited from his grandfather and used to massage his hands and fingers to hold off arthritis, I wondered, *What will Babe think of* this? When LaMu, our guide in the Tibetan area of China, told us her mother was married to two brothers who were yak herdsmen and she didn't know which was her biological father, I couldn't wait to tell Babe about *that*. Even though I was on the other side of the world, it was easy to bridge the span so Babe didn't feel lonely or left out.

My experience didn't keep me from sinking in and savoring the present moment. Instead, communicating almost daily from halfway around the world added an extra dimension to the idea of *personal* photojournalism.

In Yangshou, a sleepy rural village outside of Guilin in southern China, we met a seventy-seven-year-old woman who lived in an ancient stone house that had been in her family for 350 years. Out on her unpaved patio, where roosters and chickens scratched in the dirt, the homeowner smiled coquettishly as she modeled a "raincoat" made out of stiff bamboo fronds. This petite old woman also demonstrated that she was still strong enough, using both hands, to crank the heavy stone wheel to grind soybeans into soy milk for tofu. Inside, in a room off the living room, a coffin—shiny black lacquer with red and gold designs—was lined up against a stone wall next to a cooking area that had a hot plate, a skillet, and a rice cooker.

Our guide explained that in this village it was the tradition that when people reached seventy, they acquired their own coffin.

Standing next to her coffin, the owner put her hands together in prayer and smiled for my iPhone. It seemed to make that spunky seventy-seven-year-old, who appeared to be in excellent health, content to have her coffin so close.

The next morning, some 8,500 miles and a world away, Babe, in her apartment on the fourteenth floor of the senior high-rise community, was trying to make sense of the photo of the tiny, gray-haired woman standing next to a coffin.

I explained that, yes, the coffin was inside her house, out in full view, right next to the kitchen.

"Do you want me to keep a coffin in my apartment?" she asked.

"Only if you want to."

"I could start a new trend," she said.

I didn't remind her that she'd already chosen to be cremated and there was that urn waiting on the top shelf of my sister's bookshelf. Since 1998, Dad's ashes had filled his side.

I absorbed Babe's "*Go!*" so fully that when the first woman won the Iditarod dogsled race in Alaska, I dropped everything and took off for Nome to do a story on her. When the lava started flowing on the Big Island, I spent New Year's Eve nearby, at the Volcano House.

Luckily, when Ed and I met, Babe's "*Go!* while you can" was a good fit for both of us. We pledged to go as far as we could—always with hiking sticks—for as long as we could: hike in Torres del Paine in Chilean Patagonia; slog across the marshy Gangtey Nature Trail in Bhutan; and in Dharmasala trek in the snow-packed lower Himalayas, where we happened upon a chai tea shack in the middle of nowhere. (My brother joked that we hiked away from the Four Seasons and we hiked back to the Four Seasons. He had a point: we were in rough environments, but we were not roughing it.)

As newlyweds, we were pretty much inseparable, and we had a deal: since we'd met in our sixties, we agreed that we'd go almost anywhere together, as long as neither of us had been there before with a previous love.

Travel was our way of amassing a personal history fast. It allowed us to say, *Remember when* we *were in Tanzania, Lijiang, Marrakesh*? It rescued us from constantly referring to the interesting lives we'd led and the places we'd traveled before we met.

One evening I was discussing Babe's "*Go!* now" mandate over dinner with George Landau, a diplomat who had been a US ambassador to Paraguay, Chile, and Venezuela. I explained that Ed and I needed to do as much as we could while we still could. I felt like a travel clock was ticking and time was running out.

George dismissed my urgency. "You can keep doing what you're doing until you're eighty-eight, at least!" George should know. At ninety-two, he was about to leave for a diplomatic meeting in Geneva.

I continued to travel—usually to places Babe had not been—and I always sent photos.

LESSON 13:

SOMETIMES LIFE BEGINS AGAIN AT NINETY-FIVE

For someone who liked to party, Babe ended up at the best senior community. She'd been living at my sister's in Houston, and at a certain point my sister had started vetting senior homes—that one was too snooty, that one too religious, and this one was just right. And it was.

At ninety-five, Babe, along with Elma, her full-time caregiver-companion, and Tiger, a chubby Chihuahua–Jack Russell mix, moved into a private two-bedroom, two-bath, unfurnished, independent-living apartment on the fourteenth floor of a sixteen-story high-rise community for seniors. One reason this primo apartment was available was probably because its large plate-glass windows looked out onto Interstate 610, and even at fourteen stories up, the freeway buzz from twelve lanes of urban traffic was omnipresent. My sister figured that wouldn't be much of a problem, since by now Babe was hard of hearing. So Babe moved in with a half gallon of Chivas (enough to share), dozens of framed family photos, and probably too many multicolored afghans that Great-Aunt Alvina had crocheted.

During Babe's first week, I arrived in time to join her for dinner downstairs. (That's when I showed up in that drab black travel outfit.) The dining room tables, set with crisp white cloths, had arrangements of fresh hydrangeas and roses. Geneva, on my left, was carefully dressed in a white pantsuit with gold trim and matching jewelry. She asked me to read the menu to her. "I can't see," she said.

So this was the person Babe had told me about. Babe, who was self-conscious about being hard of hearing, had said to Geneva, "I'm sorry, but I don't hear well."

"And I can't see," said Geneva, "so we'll be good friends!"

During her working years, Geneva had been an office manager, and at ninety-two she still exuded street-smart business savvy. She explained that until recently she'd served on the welcoming committee, where it was her job to show new people around. (How exactly a vision-impaired person accomplished that, I don't know.) "It made me feel that I still had something of value to offer," she said. She also explained that it ended up interfering with her life too much because each time a new person arrived, she had to drop everything. (At ninety-two, she had that much to drop? Good for her.)

At ninety-five, Babe was the oldest at the table, and Blanche, at eighty-one, the youngest. Blanche wore her silver hair piled high in a beehive; a fringe of girlish bangs fell over her forehead. She showed me her necklace, which had a pendant for each of her six grandchildren. She'd designed the pendants and named them Crystal Children. They were a popular item at her store, Blanche Fine Jewelry, where she still worked a few hours a day.

She explained that Hymie, her husband, and Mitty—who were sitting next to each other on the other side of our round table—had been born on the same day, in the same hospital, eighty-seven years earlier. They had grown up together and served in the navy together and were still best friends. This story of their lifelong friendship had the familiar ring of one told many times, but that didn't make it any less enjoyable for Blanche to tell it again or for me to hear it for the first time.

Mitty, who had moved in just two weeks earlier, was describing his late wife, who had died four months before, as a shopaholic. According to him, she died with 150 St. John suits in her closet. Mitty had married wealthy, so she'd bought them with her own money.

But still. "She was sick. She had a disease," said Mitty. "But *what* a woman she was!" This recent widower, who still wore his gold wedding band, said this in such a juicy way, relishing the part of his married life that had nothing to do with designer suits.

My sister had said Mitty had arrived at the Hampton almost mute. That evening, he was dressed in a turquoise Lacoste golf shirt, and his muteness had melted.

Blanche ordered the Healthy Choice dinner and, referring to her husband of fifty-eight years, she said to the waiter, "He'll have the same"—except when the waiter got to Hymie, he ordered exactly what he pleased. As a new wife of barely two years, I was amused by the universal ineffectiveness of wifely dietary interventions. I made a mental note to go easy on my husband's red meat–vodka–ice cream habit.

Also at our table was Flo, who had already stopped in and played Scrabble with Babe. Flo, who seemed a good decade younger than ninety-two, was conservatively dressed—plain white blouse, basic blue cardigan. Looking over at Babe, who was wearing my favorite, pale pink Indian kurta with sparkles at the neckline, Flo said to me, "Your mother dresses to the hilt. It gives the rest of us something to emulate."

Midmeal—sole, baked potato, peas, tasty enough—I paused and looked around the table from person to person. I was surprised that I was enjoying myself so much at a senior community.

You see, on that first visit, I was dragging some

pretty heavy baggage with me. I'd been scarred by a visit to a "nursing home" when I was just seven or eight. My girls' club had gone there to distribute gifts we'd made—terry-cloth covers with dog faces that fit over bars of Ivory soap. (Exactly what every old person needs, right?) Although we were told we'd be visiting a nursing home, it was more like a hospital with frail patients nodding off in hospital beds. The sad, yellow-beige hallways smelled exactly how you'd expect. Whose idea was it anyway to drag a bunch of little girls into such a place? The patients' naked neediness as they reached out for their gifts, their insistence that the little visitors enter their rooms and keep them company haunted me for decades. It's ironic because as a child I shared a bedroom with my grandmother, the person after whom I was named—Josephine, Josie, Jo—and the person I loved best in the world. But I didn't think of her as "old." She existed in a different category—she was my beloved grandmother who let me sit in her lap as long as I needed and hold her hands as long as I wanted. Unlike all the other adults who were busy rushing around, Josie always had Time. For me.

Although I'd done the preliminary research scouting senior residential communities in Houston and several *sounded* terrific, I'd done the interviews only on the phone. It was my sister who'd visited in person. So I wasn't expecting such a friendly, smart, lively, cheerful group of residents as the ones I met that first evening at dinner. You could say they were at their sparkling best because they were putting on a show for the fresh new person at dinner who was interested in them and their stories. But over time I came to know these people, and they weren't putting on a show for me or anyone else. Also, not once did anyone at the table complain about their maladies. Whatever they were suffering from was not what they were dining out on.

After dinner, after we rode the elevator up, and after Babe switched on her gas fireplace, she said, "I met that group the first night at dinner. Hymie invited me to join them. What a break that was!"

Babe had also told me about another incident that first week, when she'd been in the pub at happy hour, sipping one of her two scotch and sodas. She'd mentioned that Dr. Bliss had said she'd sleep better and need fewer sleeping pills if she stopped the scotch. One of the residents had said, "Change doctors! When you get to be ninety-five, you can do what you please!" Babe loved telling me that story, and I loved hearing it. In the five years she'd lived at my sister's, my sister and her husband had provided Babe with everything—except a group of peers to kibitz and laugh and complain with.

At first, Babe had resisted the move, protesting that she did not want to live among strangers. She was probably remembering her mother's nursing home, which was strictly a nursing home in the old, institutional sense—no pets, no cocktails, no privacy. "I don't think they did anything for excitement," said Babe. Undoubtedly, she was also remembering the private residence turned group home where Aunt Dell had lived. "It was pleasant but a long way from having fun. Here at the Hampton, it's fun all day, if you want it." (After Babe moved into the Hampton, the name changed to Brookdale Galleria.)

My brother, sister, and I worked together and actually even enjoyed making Babe's apartment especially homey. My sister did a heroic job of furnishing it with cheerful gold-and-yellow-upholstered furniture, a card table so Babe could invite people in to play gin rummy, a dining table large enough for friends to stay for a bite. I equipped the kitchen with pots and pans, appliances, and bright yellow dishes and stocked her refrigerator, freezer, and pantry, even though the restaurant downstairs served three meals a day. Our brother installed the biggest big-screen HDTV. On the narrow ledge that served as a balcony, we arranged clay pots planted with bright red geraniums. All that helped, but that wasn't why Babe herself was blossoming in this new environment. Her fluid transition was a dramatic reminder of the Buddhist phrase, "Don't count me out while I'm still arriving."

What also allowed Babe to enjoy this transition, undoubtedly her last, was the fact that she wasn't "sick" and was a youthful ninety-five. As a friend in the medical field said, "Does your mother have any idea of all the thousands of things she never got?"

Because Babe never had any debilitating disease—not heart disease, not cancer, not diabetes or dementia, not even high blood pressure or a broken bone. The only surgery she had was for cataracts, and the only medicine she took was a tiny bite of Ambien at night. As Amanda, her caregiver, said, "Babe's one in a million." She was one in a million in other ways, too: her doctor was named Bliss, her nurse Joy, and her weekend caregiver Lovie. Now, wouldn't any of us like a dream team like that? She still had a full head of thick hair, and skin so flawlessly smooth, people asked if she'd had Botox. (Babe squinted. "Bo-*what*?") She suffered from peripheral neuropathy, which made her unsteady on her feet, but that didn't make her "sick." Back in her eighties, when she'd gotten shingles, Dr. Bliss had said the pain would be so bad she'd wished she'd died, but she hadn't, and she'd recovered to enjoy this new, final stage.

My brother and his bride said the vibe at the Hampton seemed like that of a college dorm. Since Babe had never gone to college, maybe this was her chance to experience the drop-in fun of living in a dorm. Of having Carmen from across the hall stop in the first day with a welcoming platter of cheese and crackers. Of having a social group—Geneva-Blanche-Hymie-Mitty-Flo—to share meals with. Of having neighbors knock on her door with the equivalent of "Want to play?" And in Babe's "dorm," no one had to study.

During my visit, Christel, a Dutch friend of mine, phoned Babe, and I couldn't help but think of Christel's Papa, who lived to be almost ninety-eight. The Dutch have a national home-health policy that encourages the elderly to stay in their own houses. For something like a mere hundred euros extra per month, Papa had people checking in on him four times a day, including a midnight visit.

When Christel told me about Papa, I thought that was the best: stay in your own home, in your own bed, until the end. Now I surprised myself wondering if Papa, a retired naval architect who was sociable and charming, wouldn't have enjoyed his later years more if he'd lived in a senior community like Babe's.

The next day, I was down on the second floor in the physical therapy area, riding the bike—I was rehabbing from knee surgery—when a parade of residents started drifting in on their walkers and wheelchairs.

Uh-oh. This was just this sort of scene that I'd dreaded. I was afraid it would smack too much of that scary "nursing home" visit when I was a little kid. I kept pedaling and watching, and in spite of myself I was impressed: from the woman who was improving her balance by walking between parallel bars to the man who was working out with free weights, even if they were only puny three-pounders, these individuals were still struggling to be the best they could be.

When you walk through the front door at the Hampton, in the lobby near the reception desk, which is manned by two staff people, you're likely to encounter a traffic jam of residents. At first glance, if you're like me, you'd judge this scene—most everyone gray-haired, old-*old*, relying on a walking aide—to be depressing. But I came to understand that my first impression was wrong. Over the years, as I got to know some of these individuals—I'd take them out with Babe to Le Viet, a favorite Vietnamese restaurant—I came to understand that most of them had found happiness. Not everyone, of course. Not the tall, handsome, lanky man who barged out the front door and raced down the driveway, his frantic caregiver running after him, desperate to get to him before he ended up in traffic. And probably not the confused woman who spent most mornings sitting in the big upholstered chair in the lobby, across from the reception desk, until she was moved from independent to assisted living because of dementia. But most of the residents were happy. I know that might be hard to wrap one's mind around—it was a surprise to me, too—but it was true.

Physically, the Hampton wasn't the most ideal setup for seniors. The sixteen-story building had been built as a hotel but had survived in that incarnation for only two years. After that, it transitioned into a senior-living residence with 146 independent-living apartments, thirty-nine assisted-living units, and fifty-six skilled-rehab units. It wasn't a tippy-top, super-swanky, expensive place; it was more high-end middle class, like Babe. And because it had never been completely retrofitted from its hotel days, the driveway was too steep for wheelchairs, the bathtubs weren't walk-in, and the hallways in the apartments should have been wider. But that was me, a nonresident, judging its aging-in-place design shortcomings. Babe never said a peep about any of that. Instead she asked Tracy, the social director, if she was as happy at home as she was at the Hampton.

"I'm perfectly satisfied here," Babe said. "I don't like the food, but nine-tenths of the people don't either."

Why should I have been so surprised that Babe was still making the best of it? Since social isolation and loneliness are cruelties that often accompany old age, in her new home she had a stream of spirited new friends knocking at her door. It was as if she had pressed a refresh button. For a while, Amanda, from Nicaragua, even had Babe on Latin time: they took lunch at three o'clock, tea at five. Babe had reinvented herself. Sometimes life begins again at ninety-five.

One morning I was walking Tiger, Mom's Jack Russell mix, across the street at the Gerald D. Hines Waterwall Park. Flo, who played Scrabble with Mom, was strolling briskly with Carl, her ninety-five-year-old walking partner. I don't remember if they were actually holding hands, but they exuded such physical comfort with each other, they might as well have been. And you would *not* have guessed that either of them was in their nineties. Except Carl, who was wearing Bermuda shorts, had black compression hose hiked up to his knees. From Flo's vigor, you also wouldn't know she had overcome breast *and* lung cancer. After her husband had died, seven years earlier, she'd moved from Shreveport, Louisiana, to the Hampton to be closer to her children.

When Flo and Carl circled around to my side of the park, Flo petted Tiger and gave me a hug and a kiss. I thought, *This is only my third day here, and I'm getting kissed and hugged on my morning walk. I like it.* Ed and I had recently moved, and on our walks none of our new neighbors, except for our landlady, had hugged and kissed us. I reported to Ed on the phone, "If we live to be ninety-five, we'd be lucky to live in a place like Babe's."

Is it that at this stage, at this age, people don't see a value in holding back? They form strong, intimate bonds quickly. They're living in the now, the now *now*, the extreme now. Because there is nothing else.

This isn't a new-age Eckhart Tolle *Learning to Live in the NOW*. This is the real deal. Although some of the residents at the Hampton were probably with-it enough to have heard of Eckhart Tolle, they didn't need to practice his eight steps toward mindfulness and living in the now. They were already living it. Joi Ito, director of MIT's Media Lab, coined the term *now-ist* for people working in the tech industry who are super-present. At the far other end of the spectrum, *now-ist* could also describe Babe and her new friends.

I visited Babe monthly, sometimes twice a month, and to have as much time as possible together, I stayed in her apartment—even though because of the heat I always broke out in a bumpy rash on my forehead and had a scratchy, hive-like allergy to her dog. (I ate Zyrtec during the day and Ambien at night.) Sunday mornings I got up early and walked to the Starbucks on the corner for the *New York Times* and coffee. Since it was especially quiet in the lobby, and Babe and Tiger weren't likely to be awake yet, and Lovie, the weekend caregiver, was with her, I often hung out at the front desk, chatting with the receptionist who came on at the eight o'clock shift change. Once, I asked Betty Francis how she could stand working there, because, as good as it was, it was also tough. Every week there were birthday postings but also death notices.

I told Betty Francis that just a few days before, Carl's family had hosted Carl's last happy hour and had invited all the residents. Babe and I had attended, but seeing Carl, who not so long ago had been walking in the park with Flo, now slumped in a wheelchair, dying of prostate cancer and forced to exit early from his own party because he wasn't up to the festivities, was too much for Babe and me to take. We escaped early and skedaddled—as much as someone using a walker on a sidewalk with cracks can skedaddle—around the block to Piatta's, an Italian restaurant, for fresh air and a drink.

After I told Betty Francis about Carl's party, she said, "Working here is my chance to get love and to give love." She meant it genuinely, and I could see her point.

And Betty Francis wasn't singular. I was so impressed by the staff—how thoughtful and upbeat they were, in spite of the crazy-difficult situations that accompany extreme aging—that I stopped by the office of Trubal O'Dowdy, the executive director, and asked him what the secret was. I figured they must have some special employee training program.

"It's a culture," he said. "People fall into it, or they don't." He explained that if someone wasn't treating people well or didn't have the patience for working with people, he'd talk with them, but they probably wouldn't last. He said they had training manuals for each position, but that wasn't what did it. "It's a culture of over-the-top caring and customer service. It's a happy place to work."

The next time I was down in the rehab room, a woman who was on oxygen zipped in on a motorized scooter. Riding the bike next to me, she said, "So, you're new here?"

THE LAST LESSON

About three years later, Joy, Babe's favorite visiting nurse, phoned, but for once she did not sound joyful. Since I had medical power of attorney, I was the responsible party she needed to inform that Babe had had a stroke, a pretty major one. I needed to know that my mother's needs had changed dramatically—for her own safety, she would need a hospital bed with railings instead of her king-size bed, a wheelchair instead of the walker, and two people to lift her. At the end of our conversation, at the point where Joy would usually have signed off, she paused and suggested slowly and reluctantly that it might be time to consider enrolling Babe in hospice.

"Let's play Scrabble," Babe whispered in a hoarse, post-stroke voice three days later when I visited her.

Scrabble? Play Scrabble? That was what Babe wanted to do on the very day I'd just enrolled her in hospice and they'd rolled in the hospital bed? *Okay, if that's what she wants.* I pushed her new wheelchair up to the card table and brought out our tattered Scrabble set, whose aged box was held together with duct tape.

I poured myself a glass of chardonnay and was about to make Babe her scotch and soda, when she declined. "I don't feel it would taste right," she said, making a face.

Since she drew the tile closest to A, she got to go first—family rule. We each put down a couple of desultory, no-count, low-scoring words. Neither of us exhibited any of the customary fighting spirit we employed to play for blood and big prizes. Once, I'd won a pair of black leather designer boots off Babe. I still have them. Babe had always played Scrabble like she arm-wrestled: to win.

I was drained by the meeting around the dining room table that had just ended, during which the hospice people—chaplain, nurse, administrator—had told me what to expect from their palliative, end-of-life care. I told them that when I'd enrolled my previous husband in hospice, he'd died four days later. Was this going to be like that? Did Babe have only four days left? They said they couldn't predict how imminent death was. One of the biggest advantages of hospice was that if Babe had seasonal bronchitis from the high pollen count in

Houston, she wouldn't be rushed to the hospital like last time. (She'd ended up destabilized for a week from that hospitalization.) From now on, just as she had requested in writing in her living will, she'd be treated at home.

For me, the lowest point in the meeting was when the nurse, reciting standard hospice protocol, said I should tell my mother that I loved her, that I forgave her, and that she didn't need to hold on for us. I didn't need to tell her I forgave her, because there was nothing to forgive her for. In the fog of signing all their forms—we agreed there would be no heroic measures—I was drowning. (Maybe this would have been more tolerable if my brother and sister had been participating, but they were out of town. The hospice people, to their credit, would repeat this presentation for their benefit a few days later.)

That's when I took a time-out and silently repeated my personal mantra like a prayer: *In spite of what's happening right now, in spite of the fact that I'm enrolling my mother in hospice, in spite of how hard I'm crying, it's okay to be happy today.* Because Babe wouldn't want me to sink into depression. Because people don't like to be around depressed people.

I might have been crying, but I didn't need to feel sad. Babe had lived almost ninety-seven years. She'd had a very full, wonderful life.

Studying her Scrabble tiles, she said, "I haven't played in months. Just don't like it as much. Crazy me." Unhappily fingering her tiles, she looked at me. "If only I had a vowel, an E. . . ."

Defying a lifetime of strict family rules, I fished around in the bag for an E. Not looking her in the eye, I handed it over, and she took it.

Meanwhile, other new, decidedly non-Scrabble words and phrases were seeping into our vocabulary: *aide, Ativan, sundowner's syndrome*.

I still took Babe to Le Viet, our favorite Vietnamese restaurant, along with the two caregivers it required to lift and transfer her. (She probably weighed less than a hundred pounds, but post-stroke, hers were a hundred pounds of almost dead weight.) Le Viet was perfect because the Vietnamese food we liked best—the sizzling crêpe, the spring rolls with peanut sauce—was finger food, and she was back to nibbling with her fingers and not enjoying it a speck less.

Everything was punched with the sting of its being the last time. Our last lunch at Le Viet, our last trip to Central Market for flowers, the last time we'd spread Babe's beautiful embroidered tablecloth for a special meal, the last time I'd make a last-minute flight to Houston. Babe was still here, but I was already missing her.

The worst time of day was dusk, when the sun was setting. Babe, gazing out the plate-glass windows in the direction of the 610 freeway, would muse about all the railroad cars out there. As a child, she had traveled by train with her mother; her father had been an entrée chef on the Northern Pacific Railroad.

A summer month later, she had just left the bathroom. Lovie was pushing her in the wheelchair, and

I said good morning and commented on how good she looked.

"Jimmy always says I look good, but I feel terrible," she said.

It was the stomach cramps again. (Roberto, the hospice nurse, had explained that we'd all have severe cramps in our innards if we spent our days bent over in a wheelchair.) I thought, *Okay, so maybe this is the opening I've been waiting for to say those phrases hospice said will set her free.*

In the narrow hallway, between the bathroom and her bedroom, I knelt on the carpeted floor in front of her wheelchair. The hallway was a tight, intimate space for this most personal and difficult conversation. Babe, hunched over, looked frail and shrunken in her pale pink fleece pajamas, which were as soft as a baby's blanket. (I had the same pair, same color. Costco, $14.99.) A cuddly white chenille robe, bunched around her waist, made her look even tinier. I grasped her hands, which I didn't like to touch because they were so bony it was like holding the hands of a skeleton, and looked directly in her eyes. I told her I loved her, but she knew that. Then, much more slowly, because it was so hard to say, I told her that she'd had almost ninety-seven good years, that if she felt so terrible and she was ready to go, she didn't need to hold on for us.

She looked at me, puzzled, almost hurt. "But I'm still curious," she said.

Babe was not ready to go anywhere.

That evening for dinner in her apartment we had roasted chicken, barbecue ribs, broccoli, and strawberries. Babe ate an astonishingly large amount, and afterward Lovie wheeled her in front of the fireplace and I started clearing the table. The next time I looked in her direction, Babe had slumped over, her head fallen, lopsided, on her shoulder.

Was this *it*? Had she died?

Lovie and I looked at each other, and we agreed she might have had another stroke.

"No need to call the emergency folk," said Lovie. "She's still breathing. We'll just put the pretty girl in bed. We can do that."

Lovie wheeled Babe into her bedroom and lifted her into bed. I leaned over to kiss her good night. Or goodbye. That's when Babe came to and said, "You have no idea how much happiness your visit means to us, Josie."

Then, just as abruptly, she nodded off and was "asleep" again.

Two more months passed. It was the end of summer when Babe announced, "I'm on the mend."

She wasn't delusional. The comeback kid had not bounced back—at ninety-seven, you don't *bounce* back—but, to everyone's astonishment, she had inched away from death's door. She was eating with a knife and fork again, and she could even get up by herself. This progress posed new problems. Warming herself in front of her fireplace, she said, "The nurse says I'm not supposed to walk by myself. How in blazes does he expect me to walk if I can't walk by myself? It's confusing, isn't it?"

That wasn't all that was confusing. Babe was making such an unexpected, remarkable recovery—we were able to go out for so many more lunches at Le Viet—that I stopped counting the "lasts." Even though Joy was no longer her nurse, she stopped by when I was visiting, and I asked her if Babe should still be in hospice. Joy said, "Yes, she could have another stroke at any time."

Summer passed, and by fall Babe said, "I'm getting older."

"*Getting?*" Ed said to me.

Going to sleep was the worst part of the day for Babe, and for me. Once Lovie had tucked Babe in bed and yanked up the side railings, and I'd gone in to kiss her good night, when she said to me, "Sleep with me. There's no other here."

No other here. Isn't that the terror we're all afraid of—the existential loneliness of being separate and entirely alone in the universe? "Your father's not sleeping with me," she said.

More weeks passed, and when Babe experienced more misery, when she was so exhausted in the morning, even after a long night's sleep, that she'd get up to sip her coffee and beg to go back to bed to sleep more, I thought maybe it was time to try that hospice phrase again. Maybe she was holding on for us. "You've mentioned that before" was her reply.

Almost one year after we enrolled Babe in hospice, I got an urgent call from Roberto, the hospice nurse. Everyone was expecting me to arrive in Houston the next day, Friday, to prepare Babe's Mother's Day party on Sunday. Roberto urged strongly that I come, *now*.

Ed scrambled to help me leave and tried to calm me down by saying she wouldn't die before I got there. "She'll be around for Mother's Day," he said. "She won't want to miss her party."

Just the week before, she'd attended a seafood gumbo feast down in Beach City, near Galveston, an annual event hosted by a resident at the Hampton. I'd asked her if she was really up to the hundred-mile-round-trip journey on the bus. She'd said, "I don't want to miss out."

Before the car arrived to take me to the airport, I said to Ed. "I love you, and I need you to say it to me."

He hesitated. "I like it when I say it spontaneously."

I explained that if my mother was dying—the only other person I could *always* count on to say it back to me—then Eddie had to start saying it back to me, now and at the end of every phone conversation when I called from Houston. If my mother was not in the world, I needed to hear that I was loved. (Even though Ed might have been slow with "I love yous," he was lavish with praise. My favorite was his saying that I was the best girl in the galaxy. "The entire galaxy?" I asked. "The whole galaxy," he said.)

From LAX I called Lovie and told her I was on the way. Lovie was relieved and said, "Girl, she keeps saying, 'I want to go home.'"

"She's been saying that for a while."

"Honey, this is different!"

I arrived in time to spend a sad evening with my brother and his wife. Babe was asleep, breathing so heavily that each slow exhale was a deep, low, guttural gargle. It was a classic death rattle, but I did not want to admit it. For the first time, Babe didn't notice the marigold jacket and saffron scarf I'd worn especially for her. Or her mother's horseshoe charm, which I'd pinned on at the last minute for good luck. In the darkened room, I sat next to her bed, expecting that at any moment she'd wake up like she always did, no matter what time I arrived, and say how pleased she was that I was there.

The next morning, I kept peeking in, checking on her, and she kept sleeping and breathing in that exhausted, drawn-out way. She'd defied the odds before, so why not now? Six weeks earlier, my brother and sister had asked me to write her obituary, but she'd rallied again and I'd filed it away. It seemed reasonable to think that she just needed a little more rest and then she'd wake up.

I was puttering around in the kitchen when Lovie called out, "Come, Jo!" I put down my coffee and raced toward Mom. I was certain that she'd come to and wanted to talk to me, to say a few last things. Instead, standing in the doorway, Lovie whispered, "Honey, she just passed."

Babe died at home, in her own bed, with Lovie and me nearby. How quickly she turned ghostly pale; the right side of her head was resting on her pillow, eyes closed, cheeks sunken, mouth open. The loudest sound in the room was the non-sound of her total, final silence. Her shoulders, exposed above the blankets, showed that she was wearing the prettiest Chinese shirt, which I'd found in Hanoi—pink with silver threads running through it, with a mandarin collar. Lovie must have dressed her especially nicely for my arrival the day before. Later, when I dared to peek under the sheet, her fingers had already plumped up— is that what happens after death?—and, sure enough, her nails had been freshly polished in her favorite Pin-Up Pink.

I could finally crank up the AC full blast, and I did.

My brother and his wife hurried back, and with Roberto and the chaplain we waited for the attendants from the mortuary. Two courteous attendants arrived to wheel Babe out, and if she could have opened her eyes for just a moment she would have approved of how respectfully and formally they were dressed, in crisp, elegant black suits. (For once, somber, serious black was not drab but exactly the right color.) When Babe was being wheeled out, I noticed that Lovie had wrapped a beautiful blue scarf with gold sparkles around her neck.

I could *not* stand being alone, and Lovie did not leave my side. A Southern Christian who read her Bible every morning and every night, Lovie had the most ample breasts, and I felt such a motherly comfort being held by her.

At the funeral home, with Lovie sitting next to me, among the many awkward questions the undertaker asked was if the family wanted them to style my mother's hair. They style hair before a cremation? Babe would not have wanted her final blow dry done by the Advantage Funeral Home.

Colorful, fun-loving, party-going, always dressed-to-the-hilt, scotch and soda-drinking Babe lived ninety-seven years, eight months, and twenty-five days. She missed her Mother's Day party by three days. It was going to be so much fun. She would have liked it so much.

On a previous visit, I'd told her I was writing this book. Babe, smiling, blushing, and suddenly shy, said, "Hurry and finish so I can read it."

TIMELINE:

GLADYS "BABE" SYLVIA KENNEY GIESE

AUGUST 14, 1916, SEATTLE
Born Gladys "Babe" Sylvia Kenney to Josephine "Josie" Ditter Kenney and George Kenney

JUNE 2, 1934
Graduated Foster High School, Tukwila, Washington
Received King County Schools' Diploma of Honor—
Neither Absent Nor Tardy During the School Term

For five years worked telephone sales at Sears Roebuck Catalogue, Seattle

JUNE 2, 1944
Babe, twenty-seven, married James Albert Giese, thirty, Seattle

JANUARY 4, 1946
James "Jimmy" Albert Giese, Jr., born, Seattle

JANUARY 14, 1947
Jo Ann "Jo" Giese born, Seattle

APRIL 11, 1956
Wendy Lee Giese born, Seattle

AUGUST 1959
Family moved to Houston, Texas

MAY 1, 1998
James Albert Giese died, Seattle

2006
Started living with Wendy Giese Barnhart and Irvin Barnhart, Houston

MARCH 2011

At age ninety-five, moved into the Hampton, senior residential community, Houston. The Hampton is now called Brookdale Galleria.

MAY 23, 2014

Enrolled in hospice at the Hampton

MAY 9, 2014

At almost ninety-eight, died at the Hampton, Houston

ACKNOWLEDGMENTS

I'm grateful to the many generous and talented teachers and writers who have shown me the way: Nicholas Del Banco and Blanche Boyd at the Bennington Writer's Workshop; Deena Metzger and her Topanga Writer's Group; Bruce Brown at the Olympia Writers Workshop; and Linda Venis, Bernard Cooper, and Susan Chehak at the UCLA Extension Writers' Program.

Ira Glass at *This American Life* gave me an important, lasting bit of writer's advice. We were working on a documentary, and I'd changed one little word in the script because I didn't want to repeat the word *green* in the same sentence: a caregiver was wearing green spandex shorts, and she was in the US on a green card. So I changed the color of her shorts, and Ira called me out on it. "Jo, the truth always rings clear. Stick with the truth."

I owe huge thanks to Linda Phillips, my chief cheerleader, and her mother, Marilyn, who have been early and positive supporters of all my work. Thanks to Linda's introduction, I've also had a long and productive professional relationship with Robert Asahina, the accomplished publisher, editor, and writer.

The much-beloved and much-missed Carolyn See was so much fun and so smart. She was often my first editor. I'd finish a new piece of writing, and Carolyn would join me at Gladstones or Michael's or Ivy at the Shore, and she'd whip out her pencil, sip a glass or two of chilled white wine, and do a first edit. Lucky me.

Albert Litewka, chairman, Los Angeles Review of Books, is one of my favorites, a real burst of sunshine. Rarely have I met anyone so generous, who delights in networking and reaching out to solve a problem, and in connecting authors, agents, publishers, and editors. No matter how busy he is, no matter what continent of the world he's visiting, Albert will drop everything to assist. How can you not love someone like that?

I'm totally grateful to Betsy Amster, who is everything, and more, a writer could ask for in an agent. She's fun to work with, and she's been waiting to hold this book in her hands. In spite of today's changing and challenging publishing environment, I'm so happy Betsy is getting her wish. Brooke Warner, publisher, said, "It's a charming tale of the way things used to be and probably should still be." Babe couldn't have said it better.

I extend a big thank-you to Joni and Michael Hoffman, publishers of the *Buzz* magazines in Houston, where Babe's story, in a much abbreviated form, with gorgeous photos, first appeared.

Back when I was a social media illiterate, it was my good luck to walk into the Apple store in Santa Monica and meet Johnnie Tangle. He came on board to create a gorgeous, easy-to-use, social media-friendly author website for me. For a techie guy working with a non-techie writer, Johnnie was endlessly patient and took the mystique out of social media.

Big appreciation goes to Julia Drake and her company, Wildbound PR, for her cool and original idea of launching this book with dance parties. And a huge hug to Carol Smith, a neighbor and friend, for enthusiastically jumping on board to host a dance party at her place in Bozeman, Montana, where she actually has one of Bozeman's original dance halls. Much gratitude to other generous and enthusiastic friends—Pamela Conley Ulich of Malibu, California; and Ragan Schneider of Charlotte, North Carolina.

My big brother, Jimmy, said early on that he expected big things of me. I hope I haven't disappointed him. A big thank-you to Lynn for making my brother so happy. And thanks to Jimmy's sons—Tony, a promising writer who died too young, and Chris—and Chris's wife, Jennifer, and their sons, James, Walker, and Thomas. I'm sorry the little boys didn't know their great-grandmother Babe, but when they learn to read, maybe they'll get to know and appreciate her through the stories in this book.

Also, for their generosity, kindness, and acceptance, the fabulous families I inherited from my husband, Ed: Wil and Emily and James, Chuck, and

Cassie; Zach and Wendy and Chloé, Finn, and Myles; and Ed's baby sister, Myrta, and her husband, Dave. I also hope it's been instructional for our six grandchildren to observe what goes on behind the scenes in the writing, revising, editing, and publishing process of getting a book from my little home office out into bookstores.

I celebrate the wonderful friends who let me try out chapters on them: Nanette Bercu, Lana Sontag, Shelby Basso, and Ann Buxie. They were disappointed if they visited and I didn't have a new chapter to read to them. I'm grateful for their careful listening and their smart feedback. And Karen and Arnold York, publishers of *Malibu Times* magazine and the *Magazine Times*, for promoting my writing in their publications.

Babe wasn't my only role model for aging well. I'm also indebted to my long friendship with Luchita Mullican, the Venezuelan artist, for role-modeling graceful aging.

Many writers find it crucial to have an active exercise program that goes along with their writing. I was fortunate to have Bert Mandelbaum, orthopedic surgeon to top athletes (and me!), to keep me in top walking and hiking shape. Roya Gowhari, my morning walking companion, was an excellent and enthusiastic listener, and I was blessed to have Flavio De Oliveira keeping me in shape at Gold's Gym in Venice and Brad Coffey as my hiking partner in the big sky mountains of Montana.

And a big thank-you to John Banovich, the African wildlife artist and family friend, who also knew

Babe. On a recent trip to Africa, John wrote, "Remember, when you get the chance, dance." We're all on the same page, John.

My husband, Ed Warren, is my first sounding board and editor, the first person I eagerly look to for wise feedback. I used to say that he was on my team. Actually, in the early days of writing *Never Sit If You Can Dance*, we joked that he *was* the team! He's been delighted by my progress every step of the way, eagerly popping open more champagne to celebrate every success, little and large. A writer couldn't wish for a better, smarter, more fun partner. And he likes to dance!

ABOUT THE AUTHOR

Jo Giese is an award-winning radio journalist, author, teacher, community activist, and former TV reporter. As a special correspondent, she was part of the Peabody Award-winning team at *Marketplace*, the most popular business program in America. At *Marketplace* she won an EMMA for Exceptional Radio Story from the National Women's Political Caucus and a GRACIE from the Foundation of American Women in Radio. She has contributed to Ira Glass's *This American Life*. The author of *A Woman's Path* and *The Good Food Compendium*, Giese has written for scores of publications, including *The New York Times, Los Angeles Times, Vogue, LA Weekly, European Travel & Life, BARK, Montana Outdoors*, and *The Malibu Times.* She lives in Southern California and Bozeman, Montana, with her husband, Ed Warren.

Author photo © Dana Fineman

SELECTED TITLES FROM SHE WRITES PRESS

She Writes Press is an independent publishing company
founded to serve women writers everywhere.
Visit us at www.shewritespress.com.

Motherlines: Letters of Love, Longing, and Liberation by Patricia
Reis. $16.95, 978-1-63152-121-8. In her midlife search for meaning,
and longing for maternal connection, Patricia Reis encounters
uncommon women who inspire her journey and discovers an
unlikely confidante in her aunt, a free-spirited Franciscan nun.

*Flip-Flops After Fifty: And Other Thoughts on Aging I Remembered
to Write Down* by Cindy Eastman. $16.95, 978-1-938314-68-1. A
collection of frank and funny essays about turning fifty—and all
the emotional ups and downs that come with it.

The Shelf Life of Ashes: A Memoir by Hollis Giammatteo. $16.95,
978-1-63152-047-1. Confronted by an importuning mother 3,000
miles away who thinks her end is nigh—and feeling ambushed by her
impending middle age—Giammatteo determines to find The Map
of Aging Well, a decision that leads her on an often-comic journey.

Her Beautiful Brain: A Memoir by Ann Hedreen. $16.95, 978-1-
938314-92-6. The heartbreaking story of a daughter's experiences
as her beautiful, brainy mother begins to lose her mind to an
unforgiving disease: Alzheimer's.

Don't Leave Yet: How My Mother's Alzheimer's Opened My Heart
by Constance Hanstedt. $16.95, 978-1-63152-952-8. The chronicle
of Hanstedt's journey toward independence, self-assurance, and
connectedness as she cares for her mother, who is rapidly losing
her own identity to the early stage of Alzheimer's.

Filling Her Shoes: Memoir of an Inherited Family by Betsy Graziani
Fasbinder. $16.95, 978-1-63152-198-0. A "sweet-bitter" story of how,
with tenderness as their guide, a family formed in the wake of loss and
learned that joy and grief can be entwined cohabitants in our lives.